This book presented to

_____

_____

on the occasion of

_____

by

_____

Date

Lessons from a Mother's Heart

Growing as God's Child

Pamela J. Kennedy

SAINT LOUIS

Copyright © 1999 Concordia Publishing House
3558 S. Jefferson Avenue, St. Louis, MO 63118-3968
Manufactured in the United States of America.

———————— Library of Congress Cataloging-in-Publication Data ————————

Kennedy, Pamela, 1946-
    Lessons from a Mother's Heart : Growing as God's Child / Pamela J. Kennedy.
       p.   cm.
    ISBN 0-570-05338-2
    1. Mothers—Religious life. 2. Parenting—Religious aspects—Christianity.
  I. Title.
  BV4529.18.K46   1999
  242'.6431—dc21   98-45943
                                            CIP

1 2 3 4 5 6 7 8 9 10   08 07 06 05 04 03 02 01 00 99

For Joshua, Douglas, and Anne Marie,
who continually teach me
about myself and what it means
to be God's child.

Contents

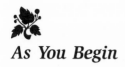

As You Begin

THIS BOOK IS ABOUT GROWING UP IN GOD'S FAMILY. It is not a training manual for parents but a collection of my experiences as a mother and how they led me into a deeper appreciation of what it means to be God's child.

Choosing to be a mother, I accepted the responsibility of teaching and training our children. What I failed to realize, however, was that through these same children, God would teach and train me as well. Before my first baby could turn over, crawl, or speak a word, he taught me things about myself I had never known. In the everyday experiences of mothering, God revealed my own character, lovingly disclosing areas where I needed to mature in Him. The lessons weren't always easy but they filled me with new awe and appreciation for my heavenly Father.

Each of the 24 experiences included here focuses on a different lesson learned from one or more of my children. Although the anecdotes are personal, the truths God reveals through them apply to all His children. After each story you'll find a *Reflections* section containing related references from Scripture and thoughts about what it means to grow up in Christ. Suggestions for personal application of biblical principles and truths as well as a short prayer close each section.

My hope is that you will be challenged to mature in your role as God's child, recognizing His gracious and tender love for you and for all mothers. His arms uphold us and His Word uplifts us. These are truly the most important lessons from a mother's heart.

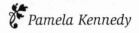 *Pamela Kennedy*

The Temper Tantrum

THE SUN STREAMED THROUGH THE PLAYROOM window, making splashes of light on the colorful carpet. It was one of those mornings when time seemed a friend and I was moving through my to-do list with productive purpose. Tiring of his play, my young son followed the antics of a busy squirrel as it gathered acorns in the front yard. He came to where I was working and tugged on my pantleg. "Want to go out, Mom," he demanded, pointing toward the window.

"Not now, Sweetie. Maybe later."

"Want to go out," he repeated with a more energetic tug.

I smiled and tousled his silky hair. "Later. Not now."

He stamped his little 2-year-old foot and belligerently shouted "NO!" with all the red-faced fury he could muster. When this failed to change my mind, he reiterated a few decibels louder, "NO! NO! NO! NO!" Then he threw himself onto the floor, kicking and screaming.

I was astonished. Although I considered our son a strong-willed little boy, he had never displayed such

uncontrolled anger. Recalling what I had read in a
child-rearing book about temper tantrums, I determined to just ignore him, move to another room and
let him run out of steam. Maybe with the audience
gone, the performance would cease.

I moved into the living room and tried to concen-
trate on my dusting. My son wailed on and his
shrieks intensified. Suddenly I heard a crash, and I
rushed back to the playroom to see a heavy crystal
framed photo of our family shattered on the coffee
table. Shards of glass and torn paper littered the floor.
Frightened and angry I grabbed up my son, checking
for cuts. Now his fury was directed at me, and he
flailed with all his might as I carried him up to his
room and deposited him on his bed.

"You will stay here by yourself until you stop this
screaming." Each word was measured and laden with
unspoken threats. I was not going to be outmaneu-
vered by an irate toddler.

However, he was not ready to be defeated either!
Now his screaming took on a measured cadence, like
the rise and fall of an air raid siren.

Downstairs once more, I carefully collected the
broken glass and examined the torn photograph. It
was a wedding picture of my grandparents and I
doubted if I could replace it. My son wasn't the only
one angry now. Listening to his wailing, I recalled the
family lore about Grandma's answer to out-of-control
toddlers, teenagers, and even on occasion, Grandpa.

It didn't seem like a very sophisticated solution,

but at this point, I was grasping at straws. I poured about half a cup of cold water in a plastic glass and marched back to my screaming child.

"If you don't stop that this instant, I'm going to throw this in your face!" I announced. He looked me in the eye and let out a mighty shriek.

As if propelled by the sound, I dashed the icy water in his red little face. He gasped and looked at me with complete shock. Tears and dripping water ran down his chin and onto his T-shirt. His chubby little hands plucked at the wet fabric as he pulled it away from his chest. "You got me all wet!" he sputtered.

"I told you I would," I replied.

"I don't like getting wet!" he continued with a whimper.

"And I don't like temper tantrums," I countered sternly.

"Mommy ..." he sobbed, reaching out to me.

I gathered him in my arms as he buried his face in my neck and cried. His anger was spent, but the terror accompanying it lingered. Exhausted by his own fury and unsettled by my response, he clung to me as we rocked back and forth on his bed. Slowly I felt my own frustration drain away as well. Uncertainty sat between us—both of us were a bit unsure about what would happen next. It was as if an angry beast had run rampant through our relationship, clawing and tearing the fabric of trust as he went.

Reflections

Thinking about my son's tantrum later, I realized I had observed raw, unfiltered anger. There was no veneer of respectability, no patina of righteous indignation. And it made me ponder the nature of anger itself. Uncontrolled anger is like a coiled snake, waiting for an opportunity to strike. When finally the angry words come tumbling out, their venom poisons all who hear them. If the words are accompanied by uncontrolled actions, people and property are wounded or destroyed as well. Headlines attest to the cost of uncontrolled anger—broken families, battered spouses, abused children, burned cities, murdered neighbors—all victims of someone's temper tantrum.

When I allow anger to build within my heart, I risk becoming its victim too, for uncontrolled anger damages the one who expresses it as much as those toward whom it is directed.

Knowing the destructive nature of anger, God offers His children many examples in Scripture. From them we learn not only the consequences of anger on ourselves and others, but how it affects our relationship with God as well.

Early in the story of the first family, anger simmered in the heart of Adam and Eve's eldest son. In His mercy, God spoke to Cain about it, warning him that his sin of anger was like a ravenous beast "crouching at your door; it desires to have you, but you must master it" (Genesis 4:7b). Ignoring God's warning, Cain acted on his anger, murdering his younger brother. Uncontrolled anger took the life of Abel, brought grief upon his parents, and God's curse upon Cain. Sin struck a deadly blow.

The power of anger to wreak havoc is described vividly in Solomon's Proverbs:

Proverbs 15:18—
A hot-tempered man stirs up dissension.

Proverbs 27:4—
Anger is cruel and fury overwhelming.

Proverbs 29:22—
An angry man stirs up dissension, and a hot-tempered one commits many sins.

Just as my child destroyed a special keepsake with his anger, my furious words and actions could shatter a friendship or break fellowship with a sister or brother in Christ. When my remarks are directed by anger, their intent is not to heal, but to hurt another. I don't care about anything or anyone else as much as I do about venting my feelings. Somebody needs to pay for the way I feel!

But broken relationships with others are just the beginning of the problems my expressed anger causes. Just as my son and I experienced a period of separation and discipline before our fellowship was restored through repentance, I can expect to experience a brokenness in my fellowship with my heavenly Father when I determine to harbor anger. When I listen only to the voice of my anger, how can I hear the still small voice of God's Holy Spirit? When my mind is filled with angry words of retribution and resentment, how can I recall the words of my Lord in the Scriptures? The beast waits to be loosed and I find my own resources aren't always enough to restrain it.

In His unlimited understanding of human nature, God recognizes the inevitability of angry feelings, and gives us guidance for dealing with them. In both Old and New Testaments He reminds His children to deal with anger before it deals with them.

Proverbs 17:14—
Starting a quarrel is like breaching a dam; so drop the matter before a dispute breaks out.

Ephesians 4:26–27—
"In your anger do not sin": Do not let the sun go down while you are still angry, and do not give the devil a foothold.

I like to think of it as keeping short accounts, of declawing the beast. When feelings of anger begin, I need to recall the words of wisdom from Scripture. Instead of conversing with myself (I usually reinforce my anger as justifiable), or dashing out to vent my fury on another person,

I need to initiate a prayer conversation with God. As I pour out my feelings of anger to Him, I experience a release of frustration. The Holy Spirit frees me to be still and listen to Him. As He reveals His way to me, I feel as if He pours the cooling water of patience, forgiveness, and reason on the flame of my anger. Certainly, the issue may need to be addressed with the appropriate person, but not in the dam-bursting style of a temper tantrum. He reminds me of His instructions to keep my anger from becoming sin.

I see in my child's temper tantrums a picture of how I must sometimes look to God. When I fume and fuss about a circumstance I can't control; when I become angry and lash out at someone out of spite; when I use my words and actions to exact revenge on someone who has hurt me, how different am I from a 2-year-old flailing on the playroom floor?

Scripture for Further Meditation

My dear brothers, take note of this: Everyone should be quick to listen, slow to speak and slow to become angry, for man's anger does not bring about the righteous life that God desires. James 1:19–20

Practical Application

This week, when you are tempted to lose your temper and express yourself with angry words or actions, stop and ask yourself these questions:

1. *Am I angry because I have not truly listened with openness?*
2. *Will my expressed anger make the situation better or worse?*
3. *Is there a way to share my feelings without causing hurt?*
4. *How can this situation be used to bring glory to God?*

Prayer

Help me resist the temptation to have a temper tantrum, Lord. Help me deal with my angry feelings in ways that will heal instead of hurt. Thank You for understanding me so well and for giving me guidance in Your Word. Amen.

Whining

THE OLDER CHILDREN WERE FINALLY OUT THE DOOR and off to school. I poured a cup of coffee and sank with a sigh into the rocking chair in the corner of the kitchen. The morning rush of missing homework papers, hair that refused to behave, mismatched socks, and normal childhood complaints about every-thing from teachers to tetherball rules left me breath-less. I cherished my little oasis of quiet as I slowly rocked back and forth.

From the corner of my eye, I spied my 4-year-old daughter descending the stairs. She dragged her favorite stuffed bear behind her, bumping his grin-ning face on each step. Reaching the bottom of the stairs, my daughter looked up and saw me smiling at her. When I opened my arms in a beckoning gesture, she rushed into them and we rocked, hugging, for a few moments together. Anne was a sweet child—the baby—and fairly easygoing. She and I enjoyed spend-ing time together.

Today we had errands to run and a playdate with one of Anne's friends. I hated to end our quiet time of togetherness, but we needed to get moving.

I prepared a scrambled egg and some toast and set it before my daughter.

"Let's eat it right up, so we can get going, Sweetie."

Anne eyed her breakfast with a frown. "I don't like these eggs," she complained. "I want sunny sides up."

"You can have sunny sides up tomorrow. Today they're scrambled," I replied, rinsing the dishes at the sink.

"But I don't want them like this." Her tone rose and fell with a familiar whine.

"OK, don't eat them then."

"But I'm hungry."

"Then eat your eggs." I was not tossing out a perfectly good breakfast, nor catering to a picky eater. Besides, I had the feeling that this was not so much about eggs as it was about having control.

Anne continued to complain, pushed her scrambled eggs around a while, ate a few bites of toast, and finally nibbled on a forkful of eggs. After about 15 minutes, I picked up her plate and tossed the cold food in the trash.

The rest of the morning followed the same pattern. Anne whined about sitting in her car seat, begged for everything we passed in the supermarket, and complained when I dropped her off at her friend's home. It seemed that every word she uttered came out in a tone laden with discontent. When I picked her up an hour or so later, things weren't much better. She grumbled that her friend, Jessie, had better toys and prettier dolls and demanded to know why she couldn't have a play-room like theirs.

By the time I tucked my little malcontent into bed that night, I had long since lost the warm cozy feel-ing we shared early in the morning as we rocked together. Her incessant whining had worn away at my contentment like dripping water wears stone. In its place I sensed a crevice of resentment forming, deepening with each new complaint. Her dissatisfac-tion was contagious. It cast shadows on all the bright places of our day, stealing the joy bit by bit. And here in the night, the darkness of discontent overwhelmed memories of happy times. How easily the shadows chased away the sun.

Reflections

Contemplating the effects of my child's attitude, I realized the subtle, yet strong influence her whining had on her normally cheerful disposition. Anne's complaints kept her from enjoying the blessings that surrounded her. Instead of being thankful for her good food, abundance of toys, loving family, and dear playmate, she chose to focus on the things she lacked. And as she did so, she became an unhappy grumbler! Her whole perspective changed and her joy vanished, chased by the black clouds of discontent.

But she was not the only one affected by her attitude. It spread to the rest of us too. Her brothers were less willing to play with her when she whined. I suspect her visit with Jessie was not as fun as it might have been either. And I know I felt less willing to give and take with her when she was in one of these complaining moods.

It is not pleasant to live with a whiner but it is something we aren't surprised to see in a young child. What happens, however, when an adult displays this irritating trait? When we allow a complaining, discontented spirit to become a habit? It's easy to do in a world that encourages us to always want more, to try something new, to be continually dissatisfied with what we have, whether it's our toothpaste or our spouse! But when I choose to focus on what I do not have, whining and complaining about my lot in life, I tread on very dangerous ground. God spoke sternly to His children who refused to be satisfied with their blessings.

After they were miraculously preserved through the Passover, delivered by the hand of God through the parted waters of the sea, protected in the scorching wilderness, nourished with manna from heaven, and satisfied with water from a rock, the Israelites raised their voices in a collective whine:

All the Israelites grumbled against Moses and Aaron, and the whole assembly said to them, "If only we had died in Egypt! Or in this desert!

> *Why is the Lord bringing us to this land only to let us fall by the sword? Our wives and children will be taken as plunder. Wouldn't it be better for us to go back to Egypt?" And they said to each other, "We should choose a leader and go back to Egypt." Numbers 14:2–4*

Although this wasn't the first time they had complained, it marked the culmination of their discontent. Time after time, God delivered them and answered their prayers, yet they refused to be satisfied. Even though the people directed their accusations at Moses and Aaron, God saw them as directed toward Him.

> *The Lord said to Moses, "How long will these people treat Me with contempt? How long will they refuse to believe in Me, in spite of all the miraculous signs I have performed among them?" … "How long will this wicked community grumble against Me? I have heard the complaints of these grumbling Israelites." Numbers 14:11, 27*

In His mercy and grace, God answered prayers and performed miracles for His people, yet they refused to remember His blessings when faced with a new challenge or desire. Eventually, the Scriptures tell us, God judged the murmuring Israelites and withheld the very thing they longed for most: rest in the Promised Land. Their constant complaining cost them the contentment they so desired. Instead, they wandered in the wilderness for the remainder of their lives, unfulfilled and unsettled.

In the New Testament, Paul encountered the same spirit of complaint and dissatisfaction among early Christians and told them to "Do everything without complaining or arguing, so that you may become blameless and pure, children of God without fault in a crooked and depraved generation"(Philippians 2:14–15). Why does our whining and complaining upset God? Why does it have such an impact upon our spiritual life?

Just as my child's grumbling transmitted her lack of trust and appreciation to me, my complaints reflect my doubts about God's goodness. After all, if I complain that my life is not the way I'd like it to be, am I not really saying, "God, You have not done a very good job here. After all, if You truly cared about me and my concerns, You would have provided the things I want!" In this attitude I focus my attention not upon what God has done through Jesus Christ to secure my salvation or what He is doing today in my life, but on what He has not done. And when I do this, I display a selfish ingratitude that diminishes my contentment and increases my dissatisfaction. And that's the root cause of a whining spirit—ingratitude.

When ruled by discontent, we not only make ourselves miserable, we spread our unhappiness throughout our relationships—including our relationship with God. We overlook His blessings, grace, and goodness, concentrating on the things we lack.

God's abiding presence is in all situations and, in His perfect timing, He provides all we need. It is the faith He gives us that breaks the cycle of complaining. When we give thanks for what we have rather than grumble about what we lack, we travel down the road to contentment. It isn't always an easy journey, but it can be accomplished with the Lord's help.

Scripture for Further Meditation

I have learned to be content whatever the circumstances. I know what it is to be in need, and I know what it is to have plenty. I have learned the secret of being content in any and every situation, whether well fed or hungry, whether living in plenty or in want. I can do everything through Him who gives me strength. Philippians 4:11–13

Practical Application

This week, determine to give thanks to God each day for at least three ways He has blessed you. Write these blessings down and when you are tempted to complain about something, stop and read through your list first.

Prayer

Give me eyes to see and a heart to appreciate
the gift of Your presence and abiding love, dear Lord.
Teach me that contentment that does not depend
upon my situation, but upon Your grace. You have
given me a gift for which I can always be thankful—
the gift of salvation in Jesus Christ. Help me daily
remember and praise You for this eternal gift. Amen.

The Too-Hard Toy

THE BIRTHDAY PARTY WAS A GREAT SUCCESS!
Six little playmates came to celebrate our son's third
birthday. Balloons and streamers, cake crumbs, and
empty juice cups littered the dining room, a mute testimony of a very happy birthday. In the now-quiet
playroom, the birthday boy played with his gifts. As I
picked up paper scraps, I heard a loud banging and
went to the doorway to see what was happening. My
son had a red and blue toy in his hands and was
smacking it against the floor. The toy was one of
those plastic ball-type structures with holes of different shapes all around the outside. The floor was littered with yellow plastic blocks—triangles, squares,
circles, stars, and crescents—shaped to match a cor-
responding hole in the hollow ball. It was clear
Joshua had not been able to get even one of the
blocks into its proper place and his frustration
increased with each failed attempt.

"Hey Josh," I called from my vantage point by the
doorway, "Do you want some help with that toy?"

He looked at me briefly, then shook his head and
retorted, "No, I can do it myself."

I went back to my clean-up chores and hauled a bag of trash out to the garage. When I returned, the volume from the playroom had increased. Josh was standing up, bracing the ball against the couch, while pushing and twisting the uncooperative yellow blocks into the holes. But his success rate was still zero. He huffed and puffed and grunted loudly as his little knuckles whitened with the effort. Suddenly he flung the ball across the room. It skidded across the floor, careened off the toy box, and spun to a slow stop in a corner. He stared at it glumly, his fists clenched and face red.

"I don't like that toy!" he announced with finality.

"Oh, come on. Let's do it together. Maybe I can show you how it works." I walked over and picked up the offending ball.

"No!" he repeated. "I can't do it and I don't like it! It's too hard." He grabbed his teddy bear off the couch and ran out of the room. In a moment I heard his bedroom door slam.

I sat on the toy box and gathered up the yellow plastic blocks. One by one I dropped them into their appropriate holes. Crescents, stars, and squares all slipped in easily, falling noisily into the center of the red and blue ball. I turned the toy over in my hands, trying to see it through my son's 3-year-old eyes.

What a mystery it must be to him. His fingers could grasp both ball and blocks. The holes were there for the blocks to fall into. He knew they were supposed to fit. Yet all his energy and effort, all his desire and intellect were not sufficient to accomplish the task. And he refused help. He insisted upon doing it himself and doomed himself to failure—at least for now.

I smiled wryly thinking of my son's determination because it reminded me of myself at times. How often, when faced with frustration over a problem or relationship, do I keep trying to fix it myself, trying first one solution, then another? And how often do I, like my strong-willed son, resist the help available from the Lord, insisting *I'd rather do it myself*?

Reflections

My son received a lovely gift—one that challenged and certainly could have delighted him, had he learned to use it properly. There was no doubt he wanted to enjoy it. He spent quite a bit of time trying to master it, but in the end, he needed help. The problem the gift presented was just too difficult for his 3-year-old skills to solve alone. And there I was, ready and willing to help him, fully capable of untangling the mystery of the ball and blocks. His refusal of my assistance left him unhappy and overwhelmed. In the end, he deserted his gift and the one who could help him and chose to suffer his disappointment in self-pity and solitude.

There are times I see myself in the same predicament with God, when I face a challenge that tantalizes me with its complexity. Perhaps it is a new friend, a difficult task at work or in the church, a relationship that needs some fine-tuning or a perplexing situation within my family. I may even pray for guidance and seek wisdom from the Scriptures, but all too frequently I set my mental wheels in motion, independently working on a solution that seems good to me. I like action. After all, doesn't our society praise those who demonstrate a can-do attitude and individual initiative?

It's very tempting to try to maneuver a situation, or people, into a position that seems good to me, one that will resolve the conflict or problem I face. What I fail to appreciate, however, is that I am like my son. I lack the skills and insights, the wisdom and understanding I need. So I madly jam square blocks into round holes, becoming increasingly frustrated when they won't go, all the while ignoring the Lord who stands willing to give me a hand. My creativity is finite; His is infinite. My experience is limited; His is unlimited. My wisdom is flawed; His is perfect. What is it that keeps me from seeking and accepting His help from the outset? I believe it is the same thing that caused my son to resist me. It is the desire, rooted in pride, to *do it myself.*

This independent, stubborn spirit is not unique to me. The Scriptures are full of examples of the same kind of people—people who wanted to be the Lord's children, but thought they could handle life on their own. In some cases, it led them to make poor decisions, in others to act rashly, and still others, to fall into depression.

When King Saul found himself in a threatening military situation, he gathered his troops at Gilgal as instructed and waited for the Prophet Samuel to offer sacrifices in obedience to God. Samuel told Saul he would arrive on the seventh day, but Saul felt the pressure of his soldiers' fears, his enemies' threats, and his own doubts. Instead of seeking God's help through prayer, Saul decided he could wait no longer. Impatient and headstrong, he offered up the sacrifices himself, taking on Samuel's role of prophet and priest. As the smoke from the sacrificial fires cleared, who should appear on the horizon but the prophet himself, filled with righteous anger:

"You acted foolishly," Samuel said. "You have not kept the command the LORD your God gave you; if you had, He would have established your kingdom over Israel for all time. But now your kingdom will not endure; the LORD has sought out a man after His own heart and appointed him leader of His people, because you have not kept the LORD's command."
1 Samuel 13:13–14

Saul eventually lost his kingdom and blessing because he insisted upon doing things his own way instead of God's.

In the New Testament we see another headstrong do-it-yourselfer, the apostle Peter. Time after time,

> *Peter replied, "Even if all
> fall away on account of
> You, I never will."*
> *Matthew 26:33*
>
> *And just two verses later:*
>
> *But Peter declared,
> "Even if I have to die
> with You, I will never
> disown You."*
> *Matthew 26:35*

Peter rushes into situations, speaks up without thinking or tries to solve problems without seeking guidance from the Lord. Perhaps the most poignant example of this is when Peter, hearing of Jesus' imminent betrayal by one of the disciples, declares his undying devotion:

Peter truly believed he could defend his faith by himself. Yet, when challenged by a young servant just a few hours later, he vehemently denied even knowing Jesus. Peter's power to face the temptation of fear was insufficient and, because he neglected to seek God's help, he failed and experienced deep disappointment. It is important to note, however, that Peter, unlike Saul, was reconciled with God and lived the remainder of his life in prayerful dependence upon the guidance and direction of the Holy Spirit.

I may not be a king or an apostle, but I too face the challenge to take my life into my own hands, succumbing to fear, impatience, or some other emotion to act without seeking guidance from God. When I act on my own, I often make things worse instead of better, not because I want to, but because I don't know what is best. Solomon, the man the Bible says had more wisdom than any other, put it this way in Proverbs 16:25:

> *There is a way that seems right to a man, but in the end it leads to death.*

My own solutions may not lead to physical death, but they can lead to the death of a friendship, hope, or even joy when they are independent of divine guidance.

How much better things turn out when I pray and read the Scriptures before making important decisions, when I seek God's wisdom before acting or speaking. In turning to my Father for help, I do not diminish myself. In fact, I am more capable of handling my life because I am no longer limited by my own meager experiences and knowledge. I am directed by the wisdom of God, the One whose ways are perfect.

Scripture for Further Meditation

Show me Your ways, O Lord, teach me Your paths; guide me in Your truth and teach me, for You are God my Savior, and my hope is in You all day long. ... Good and upright is the Lord; therefore He instructs sinners in His ways. He guides the humble in what is right and teaches them His way. Psalm 25:4–5, 8–9

Practical Application

Write down a decision you are now considering, a relationship about which you are concerned, or a situation that perplexes you. Each day this week, spend some time in prayer. Instead of telling God about the resolution you desire, humbly ask Him to give you guidance. Then prayerfully read your Bible, listening for the still small voice of God to speak to your mind as you seek His wisdom.

Prayer

Dear Lord, I confess I am too often anxious to do things myself and too often reluctant to seek Your guidance. Will You help me to lift up my concerns to You before I act or speak so I can learn what You would have me do or say? I thank You that You have promised to guide me as a loving Father. Amen.

The Accident

I PUTTERED AROUND THE KITCHEN, cleaning up the clutter from my dinner preparation. Outside, the sky was gray and a cold wind clattered the bare oak branches against the edge of the roof. The pot of soup bubbling on the back burner filled the room with tantalizing aromas. I could almost taste the hearty broth and thought how good it would be on this cold fall evening. When the phone rang, I hurried to dry my hands and then picked up the receiver.

"Mom, you're not going to believe what happened." My older son's voice had an unfamiliar tremor to it.

Intuitively, I knew. "You had an accident," I replied, striving for a calm tone. "Are you OK? Is anyone else hurt?"

"I'm all right and the other guy is too, but Mom I really wrecked the car."

I asked for information about his location, then told him I'd be right there. When I pulled up to the accident site, my 17-year-old son and another man were talking with a policeman. Our van sported a crushed door and deep scrapes along the length of the right side. The left front of the other car was badly crumpled as well.

I held back my inclination to rush into the middle of things. When the policeman went to his car, my son walked over, shoulders slumped and eyes downcast. He related how he had been impatient and when the car ahead of him stopped to make a turn he swerved, crossing a double yellow line, in order to pass. The car turned left, not right as our son anticipated, crashing into the van.

"It was my fault, Mom. I was sure he was turning right. I don't know what happened."

I knew what happened and bit my tongue. He was in a hurry, always in a hurry. He didn't think beyond what he wanted to do and he had been careless. Part of me wanted to lay on the guilt, to make him feel more sorry than he already did. Part of me wanted to embrace him and tell him everything would be all right. In the end, I did neither. He constantly complained about being treated like a child and just that morning had grumbled about not having any adult privileges. When the police officer called him over to the squad car, I resisted the urge to follow. It was time for him to enjoy some of those adult privileges he was so concerned about.

From my vantage point, I couldn't discern their conversation but it was clear the officer was giving my son a tongue-lashing. He gestured angrily and phrases like "could have been killed" and "reckless driving" drifted across the chilly parking lot.

"He was really quite mature about how he handled himself after the accident," the other driver, a man about my own age said, diverting my attention from the police officer's tirade.

"What?" I responded, a bit confused.

"Your son. He pulled over and came right to my car and asked if I was hurt, then he got his insurance booklet out and followed the 'In case of an accident' directions. I have a daughter who is just about to get her license and I've been thinking about her all this time, wondering if she would handle things the same way."

"Well, you just never know," I commented. "You tell them things, but you're never sure if they even hear you, let alone remember what you said."

"Yeah. I guess we just do the best we can." He turned back to his dented sedan with a sigh.

When my son returned from his conversation with the police officer, he was subdued. We finished exchanging insurance information and when all the police paperwork was completed, left the accident scene.

It seemed an eternity before my husband came home from work. When my son explained what had happened and showed his father the car, he solemnly handed over his driver's license saying, "I don't think I ever want to drive again."

In the end, he had to work to earn enough to pay the deductible on the car repair bill, write a letter of apology to the man whose car he hit, appear in court on a reckless driving charge, lose his driver's license for six months, and pay for and attend a safe driving course. He had lots of time to experience adult privileges and we didn't need to do or say anything to make him sorry. Life, as is often the case, was an excellent teacher. Our son learned that his attitudes and behavior have a direct impact (sometimes literally) on those around him. He learned that poor choices lead to problems and responsible people must pay for their actions, whether it costs time, money, or pain. And perhaps more important, he learned that his family wouldn't abandon him when he got himself into trouble. Our love didn't depend upon his ability to always do the right or even the smart thing.

Reflections

Accidents happen. We've all experienced a situation that had nothing to do with our actions. A tree falls on a house, the lights go out, a driver ignores a stop sign, and life takes a totally unexpected turn. But many times, what we refer to as an accident is actually a direct result of our own actions or choices. When I don't get enough sleep, when I don't allow enough time, when I'm inattentive or impatient or selfish, I get into trouble. I prefer to think of these things as accidents, but in truth they aren't. Certainly I may not have intended for them to occur any more than my son intended to cause a collision, but I am not innocent, a mere victim of circumstance. Others may suffer from my behavior and I may endure hardship because of it as well. How does God deal with me in these times and how is my fellowship with Him affected?

In 2 Samuel, King David's heroism and leadership of Israel are recounted. Among the details of battles, family concerns, and personal victories is a pivotal incident in David's life. It could be argued that it all started with an accident. It was spring and King David couldn't sleep. Restless, he got up from his bed in the royal chambers and climbed the stairs to the palace rooftop. It was a warm evening and as David gazed down upon his domain, he caught movement on a nearby terrace. A beautiful woman was bathing. In the stillness, perhaps he could hear the splash of the water as she poured it over herself. Obviously enchanted by this nocturnal scene, David sent someone to find out about the woman. Learning she was the wife of one of his soldiers—a man who happened to be away at battle—the king sent messengers to get her. David slept with her and she conceived a child (2 Samuel 11:1–5).

This whole incident, it could be argued, began with an accident. Certainly David didn't intend to commit the sin of adultery when he went for his rooftop walk. A careful reading of the Scripture passage, however, reveals David shouldn't even have been in Jerusalem:

> *In the spring, at the time when kings go off to war, David sent Joab out with the king's men and the whole Israelite army. They destroyed the Ammonites and besieged Rabbah. But David remained in Jerusalem. 2 Samuel 11:1*

David's first mistake was being in the wrong place at the wrong time. His second was pursuing the woman he accidentally spied from his rooftop. Death and devastation cut a wide swath through the families of both Bathsheba and David. When God sent the prophet Nathan to confront David with his sin and declare God's judgment upon the disobedient king, the consequences of his "accidental" sighting of Bathsheba became horribly clear. David suffered the loss of his child, the guilt of his wrongdoing, and the anguish of broken fellowship with the Lord he loved. In Psalm 51 he pours out his heart to God in phrases that mirror his pain:

> *Have mercy on me, O God, according to Your unfailing love (verse 1).*
>
> *For I know my transgressions, and my sin is always before me (verse 3).*
>
> *Hide Your face from my sins and blot out all my iniquity (verse 9).*
>
> *Do not cast me from Your presence or take Your Holy Spirit from me (verse 11).*
>
> *Restore to me the joy of Your salvation and grant me a willing spirit, to sustain me (verse 12).*

God allowed David to suffer the consequences of his "accident" just as He allows us to experience the results of our own poor choices. Our words or actions might result in physical or emotional injury to other persons or property or cause us the pain of grief and guilt. It may even seem for a time that we are separated from God, but as David learned, God's unfailing love does not leave us. Looking again at Psalm 51, we learn what God's healing means in a damaged life:

Wash away all my iniquity and cleanse me from my sin (verse 2).

Create in me a pure heart, O God, and renew a steadfast spirit within me (verse 10).

When David recognized his behavior as a result of his own willfulness, he could then confess to God and seek cleansing and renewal. David, imperfect just as we are, realized his guilt and emptiness could only be healed by God. He knew he had acted apart from God's will and must suffer the consequences, but he also knew where to go for mercy, forgiveness, and restoration. Despite the pain he suffered, David abandoned self-serving justification and threw himself on God's mercy. He received the forgiveness he sought.

Considering David's experience, I see a pattern to follow when I suffer the consequences of an "accident" in my life. I need to recognize my own part in the unpleasant situation my choices, actions, or words caused. Unless I accept responsibility I cannot move on to the next step of confession, for what is there to confess if I continue to blame circumstances or others? As I confess my sin, God cleanses me—not because I deserve it but because He is merciful. Counting upon God's faithfulness, I accept with grace and humility the forgiveness He offers. Cleansed and renewed, I can face the future assured that God's love and fellowship endure.

Scripture for Further Meditation

But You, O Lord, are a compassionate and gracious God, slow to anger, abounding in love and faithfulness. Psalm 86:15

Personal Application

Do you know someone suffering emotionally or physically because of your "accidental" outburst? If so, will you accept responsibility for your part in his or her pain and ask God's forgiveness? Prayerfully ask God to show you how you can contribute to healing in this situation.

If you are experiencing guilt over some "accidental" actions or words that have brought pain to others, read Psalm 51 out loud, making it your own prayer.

Prayer

Father, help me submit my thoughts, actions, and words to You so they will not accidentally cause pain to others. When I act or speak without thought, give me the humility to take responsibility, seek forgiveness, and work to repair the damage I cause. Thank You that in Your loving kindness You will never abandon me. Amen.

But I'm Scared!

WE LIVED IN HAWAII ON A NAVAL STATION
in military housing. It wasn't luxurious but it had
the advantage of being in a beautiful part of the
world. Palm trees, brilliant bougainvillea, hibiscus
bushes, and gardenia surrounded our little house
with bright colors and delightful scents in the balmy
breezes. In the midst of this tropical splendor, a tall,
leafless palm tree trunk stood outside our son's bedroom window. Before being tucked into bed each
night, our son would stand at the window looking at
the "scary tree" while we assured him it was harm-
less. He wanted his bed adjusted so he could not see
the tree (nor could it see him!). I know the tree never
did anything more threatening than stand in its place,
a slender gray sentinel in the backyard.

At about this same time, our son developed an
irrational fear of people in costumes. We couldn't
even walk through a shopping center in December
without at least one terrified shriek when the mall
Santa was spotted. In spring, the Easter Bunny struck
terror in his young heart. And once he froze in place
in the shoe department of a large department store,

clutching my hand and refusing to budge. I couldn't imagine what was the matter until I spotted a six-foot Hush Puppy strolling toward us.

When he was older, we visited a nursing home to see his great-grandpa. As we approached the elevator, our son asked us where the stairs were. He became increasingly more agitated when we told him we had to go to the eighth floor and weren't planning to take the stairs. He informed us he wasn't planning to take the elevator. Until that time he had seemed eager to ride in elevators, dashing ahead of us to push the button for the designated floor. In the end, he ran up eight flights of stairs and met us as we exited the elevator. For several months after that, he avoided elevator rides and even asked to be excused from outings that might include a ride in one. It wasn't until much later that we finally learned why. He had apparently watched an old movie in which a group of passengers was stuck in an elevator for days while rescue crews worked frantically to free them. When my husband took our son to a local office building and showed him the emergency phone and ceiling escape hatch in the modern elevators, he finally agreed to try a short ride and eventually overcame his fear completely.

I'm still not certain why, but for years my son allowed his life to be directed by fear. At times, it kept him from sleep, hindered his participation in activities, and even restricted his movements. He was fear's victim and couldn't seem do anything about it.

It was easy for me to recognize Joshua's fears as

irrational because they were not at all fearful for me. But observing his experience caused me to evaluate my own decision-making processes. Do I make life choices because I fear someone or something? If so, am I limiting my opportunities to grow in faith and trust? Perhaps I am even failing to hear God's comfort and direction because the roar of my fear drowns out His still small voice.

Reflections

Fear is not always a bad thing. It can be a lifesaving emotion, keeping us away from dangerous situations or people. As parents, we want our children to develop a healthy fear of fire, poisons, strangers, and other harmful things. But there is another kind of fear that is not healthy. It is the fear that enslaves us and keeps us from living up to our potential as children of God.

Fearing a tree trunk, a man dressed up like a rabbit, or an elevator kept my son from fully enjoying and experiencing his world. In the same way, my unhealthy fears prevent me from enjoying the world of opportunities God places before me. Fear dilutes my joy and erodes my faith until I no longer walk the path of life with confidence but sit instead in the shadows, trembling with apprehension. From this vantage, I can even lose sight of God's power and love.

Fortunately, God knows we have a tendency to be fearful and in Scripture provides examples and encouragement to help us overcome our fears.

The book of Ruth tells the story of a young pagan woman from the land of Moab. She married the son of a Hebrew exile who had traveled to her homeland to escape a famine. After only a few years of marriage, Ruth's husband died. Widowed and childless, Ruth's life appeared hopeless and her future empty. When her Hebrew mother-in-law decided to return to Judah, she urged Ruth to go back to her own homeland where she might have a better chance for remarriage and hope of having a family. Facing her own grief and Naomi's realistic picture of a bleak life in Judah, Ruth must have been tempted to fear for her future. Who would provide for her? How would she face life without a husband or the joy of having her own children? How could she, a hated foreigner, ever be accepted into Hebrew society? But instead of allowing fear to overwhelm her, Ruth determined to trust in Naomi's God, Jehovah. In her beautiful words recorded in Ruth 1:16–17 she affirms: "Don't urge me to leave you or to turn back from you. Where you go I will go, and where you stay I will stay. Your people will be my people and your God my God. Where you die I will die, and there I will be buried. May the Lord deal with me, be it ever so severely, if anything but death separates you and me."

Ruth set her heart against her fears, trusting in the Lord. And in the rest of the book of Ruth we see

God's protection of and provision for this young girl from Moab. Not only did she marry again, but her firstborn, Obed, became the grandfather of King David. And Ruth herself is one of only four women mentioned in Matthew's genealogy of Jesus.

I wonder if we would even know Ruth's name if she had succumbed to her fears. Certainly she would never have realized God's wonderful plan for her life. When I am faced with an uncertain future, do I listen to the voices around me telling me to take the safe and easy way out? Do I return to the familiar habits of the past, or am I, like Ruth, courageous enough to step into the unknown future, trusting in God to provide all I need?

Scripture for Further Meditation

Peace I leave with you; My peace I give you. I do not give to you as the world gives. Do not let your hearts be troubled and do not be afraid. John 14:27

Practical Application

Make a list of things in your future that seem frightening. Your list might include a health issue, financial situation, family concerns, etc. Pray for God's insights as you read the following Psalms each day. As you read, jot down phrases that speak to your heart next to each concern on your list. When you feel your fears creeping back into your thoughts, read the phrases you have written down and ask God to replace your fearful thoughts with His truth as revealed in Scripture.

Example

1. **Job security.** *Psalm 62:1*—"My soul finds rest in God alone." *Psalm 37:37*—"There is a future for the man of peace."

2. **Rejection by a loved one.** *Psalm 37:28*—"The LORD ... will not forsake His faithful ones." *Psalm 27:1*— "The LORD is my light and my salvation—whom shall I fear?"

Psalms for Reflection
23, 24, 27, 32, 37, 62, 86, 91, or any others you enjoy.

Prayer

Dear Lord, forgive me for looking to my fears instead of Your faithfulness. Help me to cast my concerns and cares upon You and to stand firm in the power and strength of Your Holy Spirit, which You have claimed for me in Jesus Christ, to face each day with courage and commitment to Your truth. Thank You for Your constant love. Amen.

The Gift

IT WAS A LOVELY SPRING SUNDAY and the salt breezes from Newport Bay ruffled the leaves in the treetops. On the way home from church the children chattered in the back seat about who did what in Sunday school. Our sons were 13 and 9 and experts on all things, while our 5-year-old daughter listened to their banter worshipfully. They were her heroes. Whenever she wanted an opinion or help with some project, she went to them. Most of the time they welcomed her inquiries and delighted in being the source of her solutions.

"You know what?" she piped up when there was a lull in the conversation. "Teacher said next Sunday is Mother's Day. And I made something special for you, Mommy."

"Oh, don't tell, Sweetie," I cautioned. "Let's have it be a wonderful surprise."

She giggled with delight and crossed her arms. "I'm good at keeping secrets. But you'll like it." She looked at her brothers for approval and they just laughed.

"I'll bet you can't keep it a secret for a whole

week," the older one said.

"Can too," she replied, sticking her chin out with determination.

All week she dropped hints about the wonderful present she was planning to give me on Mother's Day, but she never divulged what it was.

When Mother's Day arrived she was the first one ready for church and could hardly wait to dash into her Sunday school room. When we picked her up at her classroom later she clutched a flat package wrapped in white tissue and wore a smile like a Cheshire cat. The family had decided to cook dinner for me and give me their gifts with dessert, so Anne placed her special package on the table in anticipation of the dinner hour.

Finally the meal was over and it was time for me to open my gifts.

"Open mine first!" my daughter cried with excitement. She bounced in her chair with delight.

I carefully untied the clumsily knotted ribbon and folded back the tissue to reveal my Mother's Day gift. It was a white plastic dinner plate decorated with colored figures Anne had drawn. A stick figure girl with lopsided pigtails clutched the four-fingered hand of a stick figure mother who sported seven long hairs sprouting from her head at various angles. The grinning pair was surrounded by hearts and flowers in varied hues and shapes. At the bottom of the plate in wobbly pink numerals was the year, 1988. Only it didn't look exactly like 1988. In her prekindergarten scrawl my daughter had put the nine first and written it backwards. Then came the one followed by the two eights. The first eight was missing part of its lower globe and the second lacked part of its middle. The end result was that the number more closely resembled the word PIGS than 1988.

"It's wonderful!" I exclaimed, holding up the plate for the family to see. I laughed with delight as Anne rushed into my arms for a big hug.

"I did it all by myself," she proudly announced, looking at her brothers for approval.

"Yeah," her older brother agreed with a grin. "I'll bet you did."

The 9-year-old, not quite as astute as his brother, frowned at the plate for a few seconds and then asked with confusion. "So why did you write PIGS under the picture?"

"I didn't write pigs," Anne countered.

He took the plate and held it up pointing to the numbers at the bottom. "Sure you did, see: P-I-G-S, pigs. Do you mean you and Mom are pigs? That's a great Mother's Day gift, Annie, calling your mom a pig!"

I felt my daughter stiffen in my arms and sensed trouble on the way. "It's a beautiful plate and I'm going to put it in my china cabinet and treasure it forever because my daughter made it for me all by herself." I kissed the top of her head and gave her a tight squeeze as she went back to her chair, but I could tell her brother's remarks bothered her.

After the other gifts were opened and the kitchen was cleaned up I went back to the table to get Anne's plate but it was gone. After searching through the discarded paper and boxes, looking on the counter and under the table, I asked my husband and the boys if they had seen it. No one knew where it was and I climbed the stairs to Anne's room to ask her. She was sitting on her bed looking at a book with her stuffed rabbit, Miss Pittypat, clutched in her arms.

"Honey, do you know where my Mother's Day plate is? I can't find it and I want to put it in the china cabinet."

She didn't look up. "It's a dumb plate."

Sitting down beside her, I pulled her close to my side and stroked a wispy blonde hair back from her cheek. "I think it's a wonderful plate. It was made for me by someone who loves me very much and wanted me to know how special she thinks I am. It doesn't matter what anyone else thinks about it. It was given to me and I love it."

She looked up, tears shimmering in her eyes. "It doesn't say PIGS."

"I know. It says 1988 and that is the year I will always remember because you gave me my favorite Mother's Day gift."

She blinked and a big round tear splashed down her cheek. When I kissed it away, she wiggled to the bottom of her bed and lifted up the blankets. From beneath them she pulled out the plate and handed it to me.

"That's you and me. We're smiling because we love each other," she said.

"I know." We hugged and I got up to leave the room. "That love is what makes your gift special." She grinned and I turned quickly so she could not see the tears in my own eyes. They were tears of gratitude for a glimpse of pure love.

My daughter is a teenager now and while she is still a loving and graceful child, many things have changed in our lives. We have moved several times since 1988, her brothers are both away at college, and we have started a new career after almost three decades in the Navy. We have celebrated many Mother's Days, but the "Pigs Plate," as it has come to be fondly called by the family, is still displayed in the china cabinet. And every time I see it I think of the love it represents. It reminds me that any gift given in love is of great value, not because of its monetary worth but because of its motivation. Sometimes I need to remember that when I feel I have nothing of value to offer to God.

Reflections

In a world where everything we do is evaluated it is easy to lose sight of the value of little gestures, simple acts of kindness, homely gifts of love. We live in a society that constantly rewards the *best*, the *largest*, the *most magnificent*. But most of us never experience the thrill of winning a medal or award. Our efforts are seldom acknowledged with prizes or notoriety and few of us receive accolades of any kind. What a shame it would be to conclude that our lives are meaningless. It would drive us to withdraw, to hide our gifts, to stay in our "rooms" where we might nurse our feelings of inadequacy in solitude just like my 5-year-old daughter tried to do that Mother's Day long ago.

When he walked the earth, Jesus constantly affirmed the gifts of love offered by those around Him. He took time to validate the worth of the giver as well as the gift and demonstrated that true worth is not measured by public acclaim or awards, but by motivation; not by the exquisite beauty of the gift, but by the love it represents.

One day Jesus taught a lesson about this truth as He sat in the temple courts. Priests and teachers of the law, students and shopkeepers, old and young were conducting their temple business. Several of the educated men wanted to discuss theological issues with this teacher from Nazareth and He obliged them with parables. Others tried to distract Him with flattery, posing tricky theoretical questions about balancing religious propriety and civic responsibility. Although He answered their questions, He knew they cared little for the truth He offered. They sought justification for their own behavior and validation of their own values. In the midst of their discussion, Jesus glanced away from the crowds around Him:

As He looked up, Jesus saw the rich putting their gifts into the temple treasury. He also saw a poor widow put in two very small copper coins. "I tell you the truth," He said, "this poor widow has put in more than all the others. All these people gave their gifts out of their wealth; but she out of her poverty put in all she had to live on." Luke 21:1–4

Can't you imagine the reaction of the scholars surrounding Jesus? First, they were probably amazed that He even noticed someone of so little social value. Women were a low class and a widow was of even less worth, an economic and social drain on her family. Second, her offering was so small it was meaningless. Those two copper coins were worth less than three cents. The men surrounding Jesus were probably indignant that anyone would offer such a small amount.

But Jesus was quick to explain that it is not the size of the gift, but the heart of the giver that measures the value of an offering. What a radical thought! Radical because 2,000 years ago just like today, people assessed gifts according to their size, their beauty, or their monetary worth. Judged by those standards, few had anything of value to offer. What were they to make of a teacher who told them even a cup of cold water was a priceless gift? Suddenly the rules were changed and those with few talents and little wealth realized that they had much to give. More important, they knew a loving God who appreciated their offerings.

We need to hear this truth today just as much as those Gallilean peasants did long ago. Whenever we give something to God as an outpouring of our love for Him, He values that gift. A song, a prayer of praise, an act of kindness to a brother or sister, an hour of service in the church nursery, a dinner taken to a friend in need all are gifts of love acceptable to Him. Many of us hesitate to serve in our churches and communities because we don't feel talented, or artistic, or skilled enough. We point to others who could do it better or more beautifully. Yet God calls us to give what we have, not what we do not have. And when we give in the spirit of love and worship, we give the greatest gifts of all. Like the widow and her tiny offering or the 5-year-old and her plate, God takes note and acknowledges our motives, not the size or splendor of our gift.

Scripture for Further Meditation

Give, and it will be given to you.
A good measure, pressed down, shaken
together and running over, will be poured
into your lap. For with the measure you use, it will
be measured to you. Luke 6:38

Practical Application

When was the last time you gave a gift of love to the Lord? This week, prayerfully seek God's direction in determining what you might offer to Him. It might be a gift of service to your church or to another person or a material gift. Prepare and give your gift as unto Christ, not seeking appreciation nor fearing evaluation from others. Rejoice in the knowledge that God accepts your gift and recognizes the love behind it.

Prayer

Father, I appreciate Your love for me and Your willingness to accept my humble gifts. Forgive me when I too often look to others for approval. Help me realize my life is an offering poured out to You daily, in gifts of loving service. Thank You for affirming me and investing my gifts to You with value. Amen.

Discovery

WHEN OUR SECOND SON WAS 6, he wore out a pair of shoes every few months. My husband was baffled by this and asked him why he thought his shoes wore out so fast.

"I don't know, Daddy," he replied. "Maybe the shoes aren't very good."

We bought more expensive shoes but they didn't last any longer than the cheaper ones. Our son continued to defy the advertisers' claims to "long-lasting" and "tough-as-nails" play shoes. Despite the price tag, within six to eight weeks Doug's shoes had floppy soles, worn toes, and uppers hanging on by their laces.

One Saturday afternoon we discovered the answer to our shoe mystery. It had rained all morning and everyone was bored with being cooped up inside. When the rain stopped, the clouds broke and the sun made a brief appearance after lunch, we asked Doug if he wanted to take a walk. Grabbing our jackets we headed out the door.

The world had a freshly-washed smell and everything dripped and sparkled in the sun-warmed breeze. My husband and I walked along holding hands, talking quietly together as our son dashed ahead of us. Suddenly he knelt down on the wet sidewalk obviously captivated by something.

"Hey, you guys," he shouted. "Come look at this!"

We hurried to where he was and he stood up, presenting us with a fat pink earthworm, wriggling in protest as our son slid him from palm to palm. "Want to hold him?"

I demurred, but my husband stroked the slimy creature briefly and then suggested Doug return him to the earth from whence he had come. Stepping off the sidewalk, our son gently cupped the worm in his hands while he dug the toe of his shoe into the soft mud of a nearby planting strip. Carefully, he deposited Mr. Worm in the ground and covered him with rich brown mud.

That task accomplished, Doug dashed off ahead of us again, playing hopscotch in strategically placed puddles. When the sidewalk turned and paralleled a high chain link fence, Doug quickly scaled the wire wall, jamming his toes in the diamond-shaped holes until he reached the top.

"Hey look at me! I'm taller than anybody!" Before we could help him down, he scooted across the links to a nearby tree, grabbed an overhanging branch and scrambled onto a springy limb. He bounced up and down on the limb, shaking water drops onto our heads and laughing with delight. "I'm making it rain!"

At our urging, he leapt into his father's arms, then wriggled free and was off once more. In the course of our walk he must have covered three times the territory we did, dashing back and forth from one discovery to the next. He found a spider's web bejeweled with raindrops, a trickling stream bubbling from a downspout, the rainbow created by an oil stain in a parking lot puddle, and dozens of other wonders resulting from the morning's showers.

On our way back home, he stopped in the middle of the sidewalk and pointed to the arc of color spanning the sky. "Would you look at that?" he said in awe. "God must really be having a good time today!"

When we got home we left our wet shoes on the front steps. Before I hung up my jacket, however, I turned back to look at the three pair of shoes. My husband's and mine were damp, but our son's shoes were covered with mud, tree bark, black marks from asphalt, tears from the fence wires, grass stains, and scuffs from the sidewalk. No wonder he went through his shoes so quickly! He didn't just walk through life, keeping to the safe, secure pathway someone else had created. Captivated by the wonders around him, he reveled in everything he encountered. I recalled his remark as he witnessed the beauty of the rainbow and I smiled. Indeed, I thought, God must have had a very good time today watching this little child appreciate His creation.

We stopped wondering about how our son's shoes wore out, but our walk that day caused me to wonder about something else. Am I so busy getting from one place to the next that I miss the delight God prepared for me here and now? Have I lost the capacity to appreciate the majesty hidden in all the everyday encounters of life? Perhaps I need to spend more time in childlike wonder, experiencing the joy of the Lord all around me.

Reflections

Western culture doesn't value contemplation or meditation very much. We like movers and shakers, people who know how to get things done. There is no place on a résumé for time spent thinking or dreaming. We evaluate one another by our accomplishments, not ideas, and give awards to those who produce results. This emphasis causes us to spend most of our time concentrating on what we do, not who we are. Yet over and over in the Bible, God invites us to set aside the things of this world, to draw apart and delight in Him. While not devaluing our work or accomplishments, Scripture leads us to discover a balance between accomplishment and appreciation, between production and praise.

It is easy to lose this balance, whether we are employed or busy at home. There are deadlines to meet, people to help, jobs to do. Phones ring, faxes arrive, and others clamor for our attention. Who has time to sit and ponder the wonders of God?

Who indeed? About 3,000 years ago a man lived who wrote some of the most magnificent poetry the world has ever known. In it he reveals a life filled with contemplation; time devoted to praising the awesome majesty of God seen in the everyday encounters of life. Yet the author of all that beautiful poetry, David, the second king of Israel, was a very busy man. In his 70 years, he tended sheep, killed a giant, led soldiers to victory in battle, spent years eluding assassins, led his country to unity despite a civil war, organized a kingdom, established a religious center, and organized Hebrew sacred music. And that's just his public life. At home he faced the challenge of ruling his household, dozens of wives and concubines, and any number of rebellious and resentful children. Even on his deathbed he was at work, handing out meticulous directions for the construction of the greatest religious temple ever built. This was a man who seemed to have little time to even notice the wonders around him, let alone contemplate them.

David's insights, recorded for us in the Psalms, show his deep appreciation of every aspect of God's creation, from the smallest detail of life before birth, to the magnificent grandeur of the universe. Here are just a few of his observations:

For You created my inmost being; You knit me together in my mother's womb. I praise You because I am fearfully and wonderfully made; Your works are wonderful, I know that full well. Psalm 139:13–14

The LORD watches over the alien and sustains the fatherless and the widow, but He frustrates the ways of the wicked. Psalm 146:9

He covers the sky with clouds; He supplies the earth with rain and makes grass grow on the hills. He provides food for the cattle and for the young ravens when they call. Psalm 147:8–9.

For the LORD is the great God, the great King above all gods. In His hand are the depths of the earth, and the mountain peaks belong to Him. The sea is His, for He made it, and His hands formed the dry land. Psalm 95:3–5

But David's meditation upon the wonders of God's creation goes beyond an appreciation of the natural world in all its diversity and splendor. It is through the contemplation of God's power and authority over this creation that David's heart is drawn to praise of God Himself:

When I consider Your heavens, the work of Your fingers, the moon and the stars, which You have set in place, what is man that You are mindful of him, the son of man that You care for him? You made him a little lower than the heavenly beings and crowned him with glory and honor. You made him ruler over the works of Your hands; You put everything under his feet: all flocks and herds, and the beasts of the field, the birds of the air, and the fish of the sea, all that swim the paths of the seas. O LORD, our LORD, how majestic is Your name in all the earth! Psalm 8:3–9

And this is the real value of contemplating God in everyday things. Whether in relationships, the natural world, or our personal lives, God's hand is evident. Just like our son, who found dozens of small joys on a rainy afternoon, we will see the small miracles that fill our hours. Every breath, each heartbeat, the tiniest flower, the brightest star becomes a beacon drawing our attention to the One who creates and sustains us all. Focused on the amazing love that flows from God we are then drawn like David to lift our hearts and voices in joyful praise.

Scripture for Further Meditation

I will praise You, O LORD, with all my heart; I will tell of all Your wonders. I will be glad and rejoice in You; I will sing praise to Your name, O Most High. Psalm 9:1–2

Practical Application

Set aside 10 minutes each day this week to contemplate the wonders around you. For the first two minutes, read and meditate upon two verses of Psalm 148, asking God to open your heart in appreciation of His majesty. (This Psalm has 14 verses, so you will complete it by doing 2 verses each day of the week.) For the next three minutes, jot down three different ways you observe God's hand in your world today.

Spend the remaining five minutes praising God for your list. During this time of meditation and contemplation, neither ask God for anything nor relate any of your concerns. For many of us this will be a difficult assignment because we are not in the habit of doing it. But by practice it is possible to develop a heart that rejoices in opportunities to worship God through praise.

Prayer

O God, forgive me for my busyness that keeps me from appreciating You. Remove the self-imposed blinders from my eyes so I can view my world in childlike wonder. Give me a heart to praise Your name and to offer thanksgiving in response to Your abundant love revealed in everyday things. Amen.

Mom, You're Embarrassing Me!

RAISING THREE TEENAGERS GIVES ONE A UNIQUE
if not always comfortable perspective on life. There
are times when your presence is required and even
desired and other times when your children want you
to be invisible. I recall one day asking our oldest
child if he would be happier if everyone thought he
had no parents but just somehow appeared on the
earth by spontaneous generation! When he hesitated
before answering, my suspicions were confirmed.
While parental presence is appreciated when your
teenager is ill, in need of help with a science project,
or struggling with algebra, at other times absence
definitely makes the teen heart grow fonder.

I reluctantly accepted this truth with our two sons
but when our third child, a daughter, entered adolescence, I thought things would be different. We were
always close. Perhaps it stemmed from being the only
females in the house. When Anne was little we had
tea parties and baked cookies and did the traditional
mother/daughter things I enjoyed with my mother.

During elementary school she shared her happy and sad times with me and we often had "Ladies' Night In," when our menfolk took off for an adventure movie or ballgame. We fixed whatever we wanted for dinner and ate it while watching a romantic movie or musical on video. We talked about feelings, ideas, and interesting books we had read. We discussed cute boys, fashions, and whatever else caught her attention. They were sweet times and I treasure them, but it was inevitable that adolescence would change things.

I remember the very normal but nonetheless melancholy feeling I had the first time she uttered those infamous teenage words. We were shopping for clothes in a department store and I did something I had done a hundred times before. I held up a garment to her back to measure the width of the shoulders. You would have thought I touched her with a hot branding iron. She spun around and grabbed the sweater from my hands, glared at me and in a stage whisper hissed, "Mother, you're embarrassing me!" I stepped back in surprise, wondering where such passion had originated.

"I just wanted to see if it was the right size," I said.

"Well, what if one of my friends walked by? Or worse, if one of the boys from school came into the store? I'd die! I'd just die!"

When I clutched my throat in horror and inquired if she thought it would be a long and painful demise or more of a sudden, swift one, she failed to see the humor in my question and rolled her eyes dramatically.

"Oh, Mom, you just don't get it." She sighed and turned to examine a rack of earrings.

I did get it though. I recalled my own teenage despair with my mother. I loved her dearly, but I just didn't want her intruding into my life. I also remembered the dread of being embarrassed. Somehow the threat of physical torture and other dire circumstances paled in the face of humiliation before my peers. And I knew this was the same emotion my daughter was experiencing. Her need for me to be there was the same need one has for a life preserver. She wanted me to be there if things got out of control, but in the meantime, I was to stay out of sight lest anyone should think she was not intelligent enough or mature enough to handle her own life.

Reflections

As older parents pointed out to me when I was distressed by my teens' embarrassment (and as I now point out to parents younger than I), this love/hate relationship between adolescents and parents is just a normal part of the growing-up process. As kids mature they are no longer ashamed to admit they have parents and even enjoy our company! It prompts me to wonder, however, if in my relationship to my heavenly Father, I behave like my teenaged child. Do I want God to remain hidden, embarrassed by His claims on my life? Am I eager to ask the Lord to bail me out when I get into trouble so long as I don't have to be identified with Him on a daily basis? If so, maybe I am living in a state of spiritual immaturity, instead of a mature fellowship with Christ where I openly confess Him as my Savior and Lord.

When Jesus walked the earth, He encountered those who were eager to acknowledge and be identified with Him. They were anxious to call Him "Lord," and they gave up everything to be His disciples. But some were embarrassed by His teachings and His claims on their lives. They wanted to follow Him when it was convenient, avoiding Him when others might notice and criticize. One such person was Nicodemus.

It was night in Jerusalem and Jesus had spent the whole day preaching and teaching. The Passover Feast was being celebrated and the city was crowded with tourists. While Jesus drew apart with His inner circle of disciples, a figure approached them out of the darkness. He was dressed in the flowing robes of a Pharisee and he was alone. Any number of Pharisees followed Jesus around in the daytime, plying Him with questions, determined to trip Him up on some aspect of their religious regulations. But Nicodemus was different. He came alone. He came at night. And he came as an honest seeker of truth.

> *"Rabbi, we know You are a teacher who has come from God. For no one could perform the miraculous signs You are doing if God were not with Him."*
>
> *In reply Jesus declared, "I tell you the truth, no one can see the kingdom of God unless he is born again."*
>
> *"How can a man be born when he is old?" Nicodemus asked. "Surely he cannot enter a second time into his mother's womb to be born!"*
>
> *Jesus answered, "I tell you the truth, no one can enter the kingdom of God unless he is born of water and the Spirit." John 3:2–5*

At this point, Jesus engages Nicodemus in a lengthy conversation and reveals in beautiful simplicity God's plan for all people, including this lonely, frightened Pharisee:

> *"For God so loved the world that He gave His one and only Son, that whoever believes in Him shall not perish but have eternal life."*
> *John 3:16*

But Jesus, as usual, saw beyond the man's question into his heart. He knew Nicodemus came under cover of darkness because he feared the embarrassment he was sure to encounter if he asked such questions in the glaring light of day. What would his fellow

> *But whoever lives by the truth comes into the light, so that it may be seen plainly that what he has done has been done through God.*
> *John 3:21*

Sanhedrin members think? They would surely ridicule him for seeking wisdom from a Gallilean peasant. And Christ's parting remarks must have stung as He cut to the root of Nicodemus' concern:

We have no record of what happened next. It appears Nicodemus slipped into the darkness once more, embarrassed to be identified with Jesus and His message. The next time we read of Nicodemus, he is with his fellow Pharisees receiving the reports from the temple guards sent out to arrest Jesus. When the guards returned empty-handed, explaining that they had never heard one speak like Jesus, the Pharisees were incredulous:

> *"You mean He has deceived you also?" the Pharisees retorted. "Has any of the rulers or of the Pharisees believed in Him? No!"*
> *John 7:47–48*

It would have been a perfect time for Nicodemus to "step into the light" but he apparently was still not willing to risk the embarrassment of such a declaration. As far as we know,

Nicodemus never shared the truth he learned from Jesus that dark Jerusalem night.

Fear of embarrassment brought Nicodemus to Jesus under cover of darkness and that same fear kept him from publicly acknowledging the Lord. This same fear causes a teenager to act like he doesn't know his parents. And it's the same fear that sometimes fills my heart when I'm with a group of unbelievers and talk turns to religion. Silently, I assess the situation. Who is there? Do I care what they think of me? What if they ridicule me or ask me questions I can't answer and I am made to look foolish? I find I am sometimes a Nicodemus, an "adolescent Christian" who seeks to escape the light of disclosure.

What does the Bible say about this type of person? Speaking to the crowds as well as His disciples, Jesus had a stern warning for those who wished to follow Him:

"If anyone would come after Me, he must deny himself and take up his cross and follow Me ... If anyone is ashamed of Me and My words in this adulterous and sinful generation, the Son of Man will be ashamed of him when He comes in His Father's glory with the holy angels." Mark 8:34, 38

Jesus takes the issue of our identification with Him very seriously. If my spiritual life is marked by adolescent embarrassment of my heavenly Father, I am hindering my spiritual growth.

Just as my teenager needs to mature to appreciate and acknowledge my love, I must also grow in my understanding of God to fully appreciate and acknowledge His love for me. I do this by the faith He provides as I study His Word. As I commune with Him, I am compelled by His grace to step out of the shadows and boldly declare Him my Father and Lord.

Scripture for Further Meditation

You are the light of the world. A city on a hill cannot be hidden. Neither do people light a lamp and put it under a bowl. Instead they put it on its stand, and it gives light to everyone in the house. In the same way, let your light shine before men, that they may see your good deeds and praise your Father in heaven.
Matthew 5:14–16

Practical Application

This week, devote 10 minutes each day to reading a passage in one of the gospels. As you read, jot down phrases or teachings from the passage that reveal God's love for you. Spend the next five minutes in prayer, thanking God for His love, demonstrated to you through what you have just read. During the week let your light shine as you share what you learn about God's love with someone you know. Practice proclaiming the love of God!

Prayer

Dear Lord, thank You for Your grace and love poured out to me through Jesus Christ. Forgive me for the times I have been reluctant to share Your love with others because of embarrassment. As I learn more about Your love, grant me the courage to share this love openly. Amen.

Just Leave Me Alone

SOMETHING WAS WRONG. Our son lost interest in school and his grades fell. His normal conversation, sparse at best, became practically nonexistent. He seemed tired and listless, uninterested in the rest of the family. He spent most of his time in his room and when he did emerge for meals, he ate quickly then asked to be excused. We tried to draw him out, but our questions were met with shrugging shoulders and noncommittal responses such as, "I don't know," "Nothing's wrong," or "I'm fine. Just leave me alone." It was clear that everything was far from fine. I prayed for insight and laid awake nights imagining all kinds of dire scenarios.

I took him to the doctor for a checkup and he came away with a clean bill of health.

"I told you I was fine," he grumbled on the way home.

I asked the school counselor for her evaluation. After meeting with our son and speaking with his teachers, she said he didn't seem to have any specific problems, just a general lack of enthusiasm about school.

My husband, always practical, decided we were making too much of what was probably just a normal phase for a 15-year-old boy. He urged me to "just relax and wait things out."

I sought out other mothers of teens and questioned them about my son's behavior. They too suggested this was just a normal bump along the road of adolescence. Boys, they said, frequently hibernated for weeks or months, then emerged from their rooms one day like bears in the springtime, ready to participate in family life once more. I remained unconvinced but feeling helpless in the face of such wisdom and fresh out of ideas, I decided to wait and watch.

When nothing changed after a few more weeks, I chose action. My husband was helping coach our younger son's Little League team and they needed score keepers. They offered a short course in the subject for anyone willing to volunteer. Despite my abysmal knowledge of baseball, I signed up, then added my older son's name to the list as well. He, of course, was not thrilled.

"Well, we have to be at the games anyway," I offered. "At least this way we won't be so bored. And besides, you know about baseball and if I get stuck on something, you can help me out! Hey, I'll take you out for burgers before class each night."

He remained unenthusiastic, but reluctantly agreed to go along—I suspected it was just for the burgers.

The scoring class teacher had a passion for Little League. He showed us overhead pictures of score books with what looked like thousands of little squares, each one representing one child's turn at bat. He described how to mark certain symbols in the boxes, indicating strikes, fouls, hits, flies, or balls. When he got to RBIs and sacrifices, I lost him. There was no way I was ever going to get half that information into those little blue and white boxes on the score sheets.

I raised my hand. "Is all this really necessary?" I asked. "Couldn't we just mark the score down or indicate if they made a run?"

The room became very still. The instructor looked at me as if I had just suggested we blow up the baseball field. With great patience and self-control, he explained the importance of keeping meticulous and accurate records. I don't really remember all of what he said because somewhere in the middle of his speech I heard a muffled cough from my son. I glanced at him. His face was turning beet red from the effort of stifling a laugh. He kept his chin lowered, but his shoulders shook and I could see the tears of merriment welling at the corners of his eyes. This was wonderful! I didn't care if the instructor called me an idiot in front of the whole class. My gloomy son was laughing almost out loud for the first time in recent memory.

I half expected to be kept after class for remedial help, but left without reprimand with the other students. When we got in the car, my son shook his head and looked at me as if I were a hopeless case.

"Mom, I thought that guy was going to explode! When you asked him if all that stuff was really important, did you see his face?"

"Well, it just seemed a little excessive for a bunch of 9-year-olds," I replied. "I almost thought he was going to kick me out of class! How about a soda to celebrate my escape from detention?"

That soft drink was the first tiny breech in the wall between my son and me. In the ensuing months we spent time together scoring his brother's ballgames. Sometimes we talked. Sometimes we were silent. I asked him for help when I needed it and he frequently clarified my confusion over an umpire's call. Although his personality didn't undergo a drastic change, there was a new warmth in our relationship. He was less withdrawn. And now and then, he even shared his thoughts with me or asked for an opinion.

Had I listened to my son's body language and obeyed his requests to be left alone, we might never have experienced a deepening of our relationship. Driven by maternal intuition, love, and persistence, I kept searching for a way to meet my lonely child until God and circumstance brought an opportunity along.

Reflections

There are times when I am like my son. Feelings of unhappiness, loneliness, boredom, or fear drive me into myself. I resist the attempts of others to draw me out and long for them to leave me alone. Sometimes the solitude is a relief, but if it continues for very long, it may become a self-serving isolation. At this point God acts like a loving and persistent parent, showing me I am not alone and encouraging me to replace my despair with His hopefulness.

In the Scriptures, the picture of God as a divine Seeker after the lonely and depressed is drawn in many places. One of the most tender portraits is found in Genesis 17. In this passage Sarai, filled with anger and jealousy, mistreats her Egyptian maidservant, Hagar. Pregnant, alone, and depressed, Hagar wanders into the desert to sit beside the road and wait for death.

No one knows where she has gone. No one cares about her or her unborn child. No one, that is, but God:

> *The angel of the LORD found Hagar near a spring in the desert; it was the spring that is beside the road to Shur. And he said, "Hagar, servant of Sarai, where have you come from, and where are you going?"*
>
> *"I'm running away from my mistress Sarai," she answered.*

> *Then the angel of the LORD told her, "Go back to your mistress and submit to her." The angel added, "I will so increase your descendants that they will be too numerous to count."*
>
> *The angel of the LORD also said to her: "You are now with child and you will have a son. You shall name him Ishmael, for the LORD has heard of your misery." Genesis 16:7–11*

God pushed His way into the life of this lonely, isolated woman despite her desire to "just be left alone." I'm certain He already knew everything, since He called her by name and mentioned her mistress as well. Perhaps love was demonstrated in parental persistence when God asked her to relate her circumstances in her own words. Whatever the reason, Hagar responded to a God whose love she had never experienced on a personal level. And as she turned from her hopeless situation to His offer of hope, she discovered a truth deeper than her pain:

> *She gave this name to the LORD who spoke to her: "You are the God who sees me," for she said, "I have now seen the One who sees me." Genesis 16:13*

She knew she was no longer alone. There was a God who saw and understood and loved her despite her feelings about herself and her situation.

When I think of my teenage son's attempts to

withdraw into his own personal desert, I am reminded of times I try to do the same thing. When my feelings are hurt, when I'm fearful or depressed, retreating from life can be an appealing option. Sometimes I shut out those around me and ask to "just be left alone." I am thankful at those times that God sees and knows me better than I know myself. And I am grateful He is a persistent parent who breaks through my self-imposed walls with His unrelenting love.

Scripture for Further Meditation

"Though the mountains be shaken and the hills be removed, yet My unfailing love for you will not be shaken nor My covenant of peace be removed," says the LORD, who has compassion on you. Isaiah 54:10

Practical Application

If you have a child who is withdrawn, prayerfully ask God to give you creative ways to communicate your love to your son or daughter.

Make a list of the times when God has broken through your despair to communicate His loving care to you. Tuck this list into your Bible and review it whenever you are tempted to feel isolated or unloved. Make a special time in your prayers for giving thanks to "the God who sees" you.

Prayer

Lord, I am grateful I can never escape Your care. Help me remember that in my fear or sorrow You never forsake me. Thank You for Your seeking love that finds me even when I try to hide from You and for Your gift of mercy expressed to me perfectly in Jesus Christ, my Savior. Amen.

Caught in the Act

WE SPENT THREE YEARS IN A LOVELY OLD TOWN
near Milwaukee, Wisconsin, when our children were
young. When our younger son was 6 years old, he
learned to ride a two-wheeler and delighted in the
freedom it afforded. Because we lived on a busy
street and because he was predictably inattentive, we
limited his biking excursions to our block. He was
forbidden to cross the street but could cruise around
the block as much as he liked. He had friends who
lived around the corner and his travel limitations did-
n't seem to bother him. Or so we thought.

One morning I had to be in the city by 11:00 and
had arranged for a sitter to stay with the children.
When she arrived I called the boys into the house to
go over the rules during my absence. Our older son,
Josh, came in but Doug was nowhere to be found.
We phoned his friend's home, checked his favorite
hiding places, and called his name throughout the
neighborhood. Worried, I drove around the block,
searching for a sign of him or his bicycle. When my
search proved fruitless I went on foot, door to door,
asking if anyone had seen my son. I found some

older kids playing a game of soccer in a nearby playground and described Doug to them.

"Oh, him," one said knowingly. "Sometimes he takes his friend down to The Market."

"The Market?" I repeated with surprise. It was a small convenience store a few blocks from our house, across several busy streets.

Dashing back to the car I took off for The Market. Fearful and angry, I pulled into the parking lot where I spied my son's bright green bike leaning against a shopping-cart rack. Just as I turned off the ignition, Doug came through the doors with his buddy James, laughing and talking as they ripped open bags of corn chips. Quietly, I got out of the car and approached him. When I was about three feet from him, he looked up. His face went white, then red, as he choked on a chip. James, a quick thinker, grinned at me and offered his open bag.

"Hi, Mrs. Kennedy. You want one?"

"No, thank you, James. Sorry to cut your shopping trip short, boys, but Doug needs to come home with me now." I walked over to Doug's bike, picked it up, and headed for the car. James said a hasty good-bye and headed off at a trot. Doug followed me to the car and held the door open as I put his bike inside.

"I'm really sorry, Mom," he kept mumbling over and over.

"Sorry you disobeyed or sorry you got caught?" I asked, looking him square in the eye.

With a candor that made me struggle to suppress

a smile, he replied, "I guess both."

It was a quiet ride home. When we arrived, and he put his bike in the garage, he walked like a condemned man into the kitchen, where he slumped down in a chair.

I was already late for my appointment so I called to reschedule it. After paying the babysitter for her time, I sent her home and then sat down for a talk with my son.

"How many times have you gone to The Market like this?" I asked.

He hung his head. "Just a few," he whispered.

"I trusted you to follow the rules we made for your safety."

"Yeah, I know. But James said it was OK because it wasn't really very far. And I was really, really careful, Mom." He looked up hopefully, thinking this might help get him off the hook.

"James isn't your mom or dad. And I don't care how careful you think you were. You were dishonest and careless and selfish. You didn't think about anyone but yourself."

Big tears gathered in his eyes and I wanted to forget the whole thing and gather him into my lap and hug him. But I knew to let the opportunity for discipline pass would be irresponsible on my part and not serve his best interests. So we talked a little more about obedience and why he needed to follow our rules. Then we went to the garage and locked his bike up for awhile. We tossed the remaining corn chips in the trash and deducted the babysitter's fee from his piggybank. Then he spent the rest of the day in his room. When he emerged for dinner, we hugged and I told him how glad I was that he was our son and he was safe. And he assured me he was going to mind the rules from now on. I ruffled his soft brown hair and smiled, thinking to myself, "until the next time!"

We laugh now as we recall the "Market Escapade," but it remains a favorite memory of mine when I think about our children. There are so many little situations requiring discipline as children grow up. Often it is easier to overlook them or simply fly into a rage than to spend time teaching and correcting. True discipline takes effort, love, emotion, and creativity. It's sometimes hard to look into the face of a tearful child and remember that learning to be honest and obedient brings lasting joy while getting off the hook only leads to greater rebellion later. But I believe that's what being a parent involves—looking at the long-term results of discipline instead of doing what's easiest at the moment. After all, isn't that how God treats us?

Reflections

Just like my son, I like to push the envelope of God's love at times. It's so appealing to head off in my own direction, confident I can take care of myself. I listen to the voices of those around me, urging independence, tempting me to forget the admonitions of my heavenly Father. Invariably, however, I find myself standing before God ashamed, caught in the act of disobedience, holding my half-eaten bag of rebellion in my hands. Then my loving Parent takes me aside for discipline, pointing me back to His Word for correction. I wonder if God gets weary of this tedious chore. Does He ever want to just forget about it and let me go my own way headlong down the road to destruction? After all, He has been patiently disciplining His children since the beginning of the world.

Eons ago, in a beautiful and perfect garden, God placed His first two children together and gave them some very simple and explicit rules for obedience. He loved them and spent time with them, sharing with them all He had. They knew a fellowship unlike any other. Despite the love and care that enveloped them, Adam and Eve chose to step over the boundaries God had given.

> *When the woman saw that the fruit of the tree was good for food and pleasing to the eye, and also desirable for gaining wisdom, she took some and ate it. She also gave some to her husband, who was with her, and he ate it. Then the eyes of both of them were opened, and they realized they were naked; so they sewed fig leaves together and made coverings for themselves. Genesis 3:6–7*

Someone else might have looked the other way and ignored their disobedience. But God is love and love never fails. He confronted Adam and Eve with their sin and the consequences. There was punishment to endure: pain in childbirth and unrelenting toil to produce the things abundantly available before. But there was also blessing and mercy as "the LORD God made garments of skin for Adam and his wife and clothed them" (Genesis 3:21). They had to leave their beautiful Garden of Eden, but the Gardener did not abandon them. His discipline didn't remove love; it proved love.

When God "catches me in the act" of disobedience, whether in action or attitude, He proves His love to me by holding me accountable. I may be required to go to another and humbly ask forgiveness, to make restitution, and to endure shame, knowing I have disappointed my loving Father. But despite the unpleasantness of such discipline, I am never cast away from His loving care. Just as my repentant son discovered, there is growth and hope beyond the discipline. And loving arms to hold us when we fall.

Scripture for Further Meditation

No discipline seems pleasant at the time, but painful. Later on, however, it produces a harvest of righteousness and peace for those who have been trained by it. Hebrews 12:11

Practical Application

If you find it difficult to train your children in loving and constructive ways, make this a matter of prayer. Each time you need to exercise discipline, ask God to help you think of methods that will result in long-term character growth, not simply short-term punishment. When you experience God's discipline for actions, words, or attitudes that are disobedient to His teaching, prayerfully repent and humbly submit to His training.

Prayer

Father, forgive me for my disobedience to You. I thank You that You love me enough to correct and discipline me. Help me accept Your discipline with humility and grace so I can grow to be the person You desire. Amen.

Being Comforted

I WAS JUST DRIFTING OFF TO SLEEP when I heard the baby cry. The sound seemed to come from some distant place and I turned, burrowing my head into the soft pillow. Insistently, the wails grew louder and I could no longer pretend they were only in my dreams. Sighing, I looked at my peacefully sleeping husband, cozy in his oblivion. I swung my legs over the side of the bed, reaching for my slippers. Grabbing my robe, I shrugged into it, yawning as I padded down the hallway to the nursery.

Soft silver moonlight streamed through the window, bathing my crying daughter in its cool glow. She stood in her crib clutching the side rail, her chubby cheeks wet with tears. When she saw me in the doorway, she lifted her arms and whimpered, "Mama, up." Crossing the room, I lifted her from her bed and carried her to the rocker in the corner.

Settling into the familiar comfort of the old chair, I wrapped my arms around her and held her tightly. She snuggled close, looking up at me with swimming eyes and I smiled into her little face, gently drying her cheeks with the corner of her blanket. Her cries lessened, slowing to an occasional hiccup. I began to hum an old lullaby. As the rhythm of rocker and melody blended, she sighed contentedly. Reaching up with one little hand, she stroked my cheek in the dim moonlight and stared into my eyes. Slowly, her eyelids drifted down and finally closed.

I sat there for a long time that night rocking my daughter, wondering at the bond between mother and child. Here, against my breast, beat a tiny heart that counted on me in so many ways. In her little world, I had the power to chase away the frightening dreams that tormented her sleep and to bring peace. She cried out her need in the darkness and I came. She lifted her arms in total trust and I embraced her. She gazed at my face and I sang her songs of comfort until her heart calmed and she rested in contentment. How wonderful to have that kind of trust in others, to place yourself in their arms and never question the abundance of their love or their ability to provide all you need.

It occurred to me as we rocked there in the moonlight that I have One who loves and cares for me more perfectly than I do for my daughter. He is listening for my cry in the night and will come to me as surely as I respond to my own child. I only need to be willing to be lifted in His arms and to rest there, focused on Him until the peace comes.

Reflections

As a mother I'm busy about so many things that I find it difficult to carve out time to spend in communion with the Lord. I get caught up in running a household, driving kids here and there, and church and community responsibilities. In the frantic pace of life, peace and contentment often elude me. I fall into bed at night exhausted yet restless. And then I think of that scene in the nursery and it reminds me that I've perhaps missed doing the very thing that would bring contentment and serenity at the end of the day.

Luke relates the story of two sisters who loved Jesus. One day the Master came to their home and their response to His visit gives me insights into my own dilemma:

> *As Jesus and His disciples were on their way, He came to a village where a woman named Martha opened her home to Him. She had a sister called Mary, who sat at the Lord's feet listening to what He said. But Martha was distracted by all the preparations that had to be made. She came to Him and asked, "Lord, don't you care that my sister has left me to do the work by myself? Tell her to help me!"*
>
> *"Martha, Martha," the Lord answered, "you are worried and upset about many things, but only one thing is needed. Mary has chosen what is better, and it will not be taken away from her." Luke 10:38–42*

I find I am both these women—too often Martha and too seldom Mary. When I finish a Martha day of running errands, doing laundry, and fixing meals, it's easy to become resentful of others who aren't helpful or appreciative. Can't they see how stressed I am? Like Martha I want to shake my fist and ask God to whip them into shape.

I suspect what God wants me to do at those times, however, is to be more of a Mary. He desires me to set aside the busyness of my life, the concerns and fears that plague me, and call out to Him. He invites me to sit at His feet (or crawl into His arms) and be still. Once in that place of quietness, I can focus on His words and allow His peace to invade my heart. It is then I hear His tender assurance that this is the better way.

Just as my daughter sought no other solution to her problems but to cry out to be lifted and comforted by me, I need to seek solace from the One who desires to teach me how to handle my life. Many adults find it difficult to return to that place of child-like trust and dependency, but it is what Jesus desires. It is, as He told Martha, both better and enduring. And more important, it is His will.

Scripture for Further Meditation
"Come to Me, all you who are weary and burdened, and I will give you rest." Matthew 11:28

Practical Application

Plan a time each day to be alone for at least 15 minutes. Sit or kneel and picture Jesus sitting beside you. In prayer, bring your concerns to Him. Spend a few minutes thanking Him for His enduring love for you. Finally, read one of the short passages listed below, asking Him to instruct you as you meditate on His teaching. As you develop the habit of "sitting at His feet" like Mary, you will discover the better and more enduring way to peace.

Scripture passages for this exercise: Matthew 5:38–42, 43–48, 6:1–4, 5–15, 16–18, 19–24, 25–34, 7:1–6, 7–12, 13–23, 24–27

Prayer

Lord Jesus, give me a hunger to spend time alone with You, listening to Your Spirit as You teach me from Your Word. Help me develop a childlike trust that clings to You for peace and comfort. I thank You that You are always near and that You hear me whenever I call to You. Amen.

It's Impossible!

OUR 14-YEAR-OLD DAUGHTER RUSHED IN THE DOOR after school and dramatically dropped her books and backpack on the table. She slumped into a chair and put her head in her hands, her long hair covering her face like a silken veil.

"Oh," she moaned. "This is terrible, just terrible. I don't know what to do. This is going to be impossible." She slowly shook her head from side to side. "I don't know what to do," she repeated.

After living for many years with our own version of Sarah Bernhart, I was used to her theatrical responses to life. And besides, at her age, just about anything from a broken fingernail to a bad score on a math test could elicit great distress. I put down the carrot I was peeling, dried my hands and sat down across from her at the table.

"Something bothering you?" I queried.

She flopped her arms down on the table and tossed her hair back out of her eyes. "You won't believe the mess I'm in. There is absolutely no way to straighten this out without totally ruining two friendships. I can't believe it. I am going to be the only person in the ninth grade with no friends after this is over." Her eyes filled with tears.

We had moved during the summer and our daughter was in a new school. She didn't know anyone there and was naturally apprehensive about being accepted. Now, after a few tentative weeks, she was beginning to feel at ease, doing well in her classes and making new friends. I could understand her concern, but couldn't imagine what would destroy her life so completely! As I gently inquired about the nature of the disaster, the story unfolded.

The English teacher had given an assignment where the students were to work in pairs. As everyone scrambled to choose a partner, our daughter Anne was uncertain about whom to approach. Then two different girls came to her, asking to be her partner. Now she was torn. An excellent and organized student, Anne preferred to work with the girl who was similarly motivated. The other girl was apparently known for turning in poorly prepared or late papers. Both of the girls had been kind and encouraging to Anne, welcoming her into their social circles at school. If she chose to work with the better student, they would probably produce an excellent project and get a good grade. If she decided to team up with the other girl, she felt she'd end up doing most of the work and the project wouldn't be as good.

"And either way," she sighed, "I will end up making one of them mad and lose a friend. There is just no good solution to this. It's impossible."

I agreed it was a tough situation. "You know," I concluded finally, "when I'm stuck in a situation and I can't figure out what to do, I pray. God always knows a solution that would never have occurred to me. Sometimes when I can only see a way for someone to win and someone to lose, God gives me an idea that lets everyone win. Do you want to try praying about it?"

She looked skeptical, but shrugged. "I guess I don't have anything to lose."

We prayed together for a few minutes, then I went back to my chores and she got started on her homework. I continued to pray for guidance. It really wasn't an earth-shaking problem from my perspective, but I knew it was from hers. I wanted her to know God cared about all the details in her life and was always available to answer her prayers.

That night as she crawled into bed, I went into her room and sat beside her. "Any ideas yet about how to solve your problem?"

"No, none that will keep me from losing friends," she answered.

Suddenly I remembered a situation my husband and I had experienced a few months earlier as he was making a decision about changing careers. I shared with my daughter how God led us to make a difficult choice and how, in the end, all our concerns were met with positive results. "Keep praying," I urged. "God knows just the right answer for you too."

In the morning Anne announced she had decided

upon a course of action. "I prayed and I think this is the right thing to do," she said. "And I'm just going to let God worry about people not understanding or getting mad."

I could hardly wait for her to return from school that afternoon. When she burst into the house at 3:00 I could tell from her face things had gone well. "It was amazing!" she exclaimed breathlessly. "I talked to them both and told them what I decided and why, and no one got mad and the girl I'm not working with said it was OK because this other girl doesn't have a partner and asked her and you were right! God knows how to make everyone win!"

I hugged her. "Yeah, He's pretty smart all right." Silently I thanked God for answering a teenager's prayer. My daughter's faith grew a little more that day as she learned our impossibilities are God's opportunities.

Reflections

When I listen to my children's problems and concerns, it is sometimes easy for me to see a solution. From my perspective things that seem like mysteries to them are really quite straightforward. I am willing to offer advice or gentle guidance when they ask— and sometimes even when they don't! I wonder if that is how God looks at the perplexities of my life. Are the things that seem impossible to me merely opportunities for Him to demonstrate His wisdom and love?

Long ago in the dusty town of Zarephath, things had reached an impossible state. There had been no rain for months. Streams dried up. Wells went dry. Crops failed and the markets were empty. A poor widow and her young son neared death. One day the desperate woman realized there was no longer any hope. She set out from her tiny house with grim determination. At least they would have one last meal before they died. Unknown to her, God witnessed her sad plight and was already working on a miraculous solution.

As she searched for twigs to build a fire for her final meal, the woman saw a stranger. He called to her.

" 'Would you bring me a little water in a jar so I may have a drink?' he asked." (verse 10)

She must have been tempted to say no and continue with her grim task, but he was a stranger and it would be a grave breach of hospitality to deny his simple request. As she went to get the water he called once more,

"And bring me, please, a piece of bread." (verse 11)
"As surely as the LORD your God lives," she replied, "I don't have any bread—only a handful of flour in a jar and a little oil in a jug. I am gathering a few sticks to take home and make a meal for myself and my son, that we may eat it—and die."

> *Elijah said to her, "Don't be afraid. Go home and do as you have said. But first make a small cake of bread for me from what you have and bring it to me, and then make something for yourself and your son. For this is what the LORD, the God of Israel, says: 'The jar of flour will not be used up and the jug of oil will not run dry until the day the LORD gives rain on the land.' " 1 Kings 17:11–14*

The widow did what Elijah asked and the Lord honored his promise. For about three years (Luke 4:25) Elijah, the widow, and her son lived on the flour and oil God miraculously provided from her little jar and jug. Out of her impossibility He provided the opportunity for her to be fed physically and to enjoy spiritual satisfaction from fellowship with the prophet. God designed a solution where all participants won.

In the face of my impossibilities, I need to remember that God sees my situation and knows how to bring victory out of it. In the large and small challenges I face each day He will never leave me alone with my problems. As I turn to Him, seeking His solutions, I learn once more He is a God who delights in doing the impossible.

Scripture for Further Meditation

Jesus looked at them and said, "With man this is impossible, but with God all things are possible." Matthew 19:26

Practical Application

When faced with a situation you believe is impossible, a decision you feel incapable of making, or a problem for which you see no solution, write it down on a piece of paper. Below it write out Matthew 19:26. Every time you are tempted to worry or despair about your concern, read the verse aloud or repeat it from memory. As you pray for insight, ask God to reveal how He will change your impossibility into an opportunity for your faith to grow.

Prayer

Father, I know You are a God who loves each of Your children immeasurably. I bring to You this deep concern for which I see no solution and I trust in Your loving wisdom. Help me to listen for Your direction and to be obedient as You show me Your answer to my problem. Amen.

Jump!

WHEN OUR FIRST SON WAS ABOUT TWO YEARS OLD, we lived in Hawaii. I often took him to the beach where he played at the water's edge, delighting in foamy waves tickling his toes. One day, however, he chased a retreating wave as it slithered away down the golden sand. I dashed after him, but not before a second wave knocked him off his feet and tumbled him over in its frothy crest. As I snatched him out of the water, he sputtered and coughed, clinging to me in panic. He was covered with sand and a long piece of seaweed clung to his face. Screaming, he clawed at the slimy strip of kelp and flung it to the sand. In a single moment, his delight in the beach turned to fear. He wanted nothing to do with water other than in the bathtub.

We tried everything to get him over his fear of water. When he was 4, I took him to Tiny Tots swim lessons. He cooperated when the teacher asked him to sit on the pool edge and kick his toes in the water. He even agreed to stand on the step at the shallow end of the pool and let the water lap at his knees. But the day the other Tiny Tots jumped to their teachers in the deep water, Josh announced that he couldn't do that because his mother didn't want him to get his head wet!

When we traveled to my parents' beach house in the summers, all the neighbor kids frolicked in the water. Some of them our son's age even tried water skiing. But not Josh. He dug in the sand well away from the water's edge. We wondered if he would ever learn to swim.

Then one July, we took a car trip to southern California. When we stopped late in the afternoon at a motel, the 100-degree heat hit us like a wall. As we carried our bags to the room, we passed a beautiful blue swimming pool. The water shimmered invitingly and our younger son, an avid swimmer at age 4, begged for a dip before dinner. We were only too happy to agree and quickly changed into our suits. At 8, Josh still refused to get his head wet, but the heat had driven even him to at least stand in the water and cool off.

My husband dove in and swam a few lengths of the pool before submitting to countless rounds of "catch me, Dad" as our youngest leapt off the diving board into his arms. I watched Josh pensively study his brother leaping with abandon into his father's arms. Would he ever have enough courage to do it, I wondered.

Slowly, he waded to the ladder at the shallow end of the pool and climbed up to the pool deck. He stood there for a few minutes, then walked noncha-

lantly along the pool's edge to the diving board.
Again he stopped, watching his brother jump into the
pool. I stared, holding my breath as our older son
climbed the steps and gingerly edged his way to the
end of the board. I saw the fear in his eyes as he
looked into the water. My husband positioned himself
about six feet from the diving board.

"Josh, don't look at the water," he called out.
"Look at me. I'll catch you, Son. Just jump!" Josh
stood there trembling despite the heat. Then, slowly,
he raised his eyes from the water below and fixed
them on his father. He took a deep breath and with
all the courage he could muster, leapt off the diving
board.

With a mighty splash he plummeted below the
surface then came up, clasped in his father's arms,
sputtering and laughing. We all cheered at the look of
triumph on his face.

That day our son learned a great lesson about
faith and fear. He learned one can totally defeat the
other and a father's love makes the difference about
which one wins.

Reflections

How many times have I stood on the edge of an
experience, fearful of diving in? My fears might
come because of a bad experience in the past or
because of my reluctance to take a chance. Or they

might be a symptom of my lack of faith that God will be there to rescue and restore me if I fail. Just like my son, I can waste years waiting, watching, and worrying when I could be working. Blinded by my own limitations, I risk missing out on God's unlimited grace.

There was a time when the disciples had such an experience. They had just watched Jesus feed thousands of hungry people with five loaves and two fish. As a testimony to God's abundant grace, there were even 12 baskets of leftovers! Immediately after this miraculous feast, Jesus hustled the disciples into a boat and sent them on ahead of Him to Gennesaret while He went up into the hills by Himself to pray.

When evening came, He was there alone, but the boat was already a considerable distance from land, buffeted by the waves because the wind was against it. During the fourth watch of the night Jesus went out to them, walking on the lake. When the disciples saw Him walking on the lake, they were terrified. "It's a ghost," they said, and cried out in fear. But Jesus immediately said to them: "Take courage! It is I. Don't be afraid."

"Lord, if it's You," Peter replied, "tell me to come to You on the water."

"Come," He said.

> *Then Peter got down out of the boat, walked on water and came toward Jesus. But when he saw the wind, he was afraid and, beginning to sink, cried out, "Lord, save me!"*
>
> *Immediately Jesus reached out His hand and caught him. "You of little faith," He said, "why did you doubt?" Matthew 14:23–31*

Every time I read this familiar story, I think about the disciples who *didn't* get out of the boat and walk on the water. I suspect any one of them could have obeyed Jesus' command to "Come." The Savior knew they were afraid, and He told them who He was. The choice was theirs. Would they follow their fear or their faith?

Each time I face a storm in my life I'm in the same boat as those disciples. I have to choose to stay where I am and hang on or let go and risk walking with Jesus. When Peter put his foot in the water, the storm didn't stop. The waves still lashed the little craft. The wind still blew. Nothing about the circumstances changed. What changed was Peter. He made up his mind to take Jesus at His word. How I long to be like that in the midst of my storms—to launch out despite my fear, choosing faith instead.

When I recall my 8-year-old son standing on the end of the diving board, I realize he was just as afraid the second after he jumped as he was the moment before. The circumstances had not changed, but our son had determined to be different. He decided to trust his father more than his fear. He chose to jump.

Scripture for Further Meditation

So do not fear, for I am with you; do not be dismayed, for I am your God. I will strengthen you and help you; I will uphold you with My righteous right hand. Isaiah 41:10

Practical Application

Is God calling you to do something you fear? Perhaps it involves taking a responsibility in your church or community, speaking out for Him in a situation at home or at work. It may be seeking forgiveness from one you have wronged or against whom you hold resentment or bitterness. This week choose to step out of your boat of fear and walk with Jesus in the obedience of faith. Trust Him to give you the courage and the words you need.

Prayer

Dear Jesus, I know You are always with me. Forgive me when I look at my fears instead of You. Please grant me the courage to follow Your will with trusting obedience. I thank You for Your promise to strengthen and uphold me as I jump into Your arms. Amen.

Why Don't We Just Start Over?

IT WAS ONE OF THOSE WEEKS when I felt nothing else could go wrong. Then it did. My husband was on an extended trip overseas and the three children and I had enjoyed about all of each other we could stand.

On the way home from school, my younger son was taunted by some bigger boys in the neighborhood. When he ran into the house out of breath and frightened, gasping his tale of escape from certain death, his older brother decided to play hero. Ignoring my advice to just let things go, the two of them dashed back outside to "teach those jerks a lesson." Pulling on my coat, I dashed after them hoping to forestall a neighborhood riot.

In the meantime, my 5-year-old daughter was left alone in the house. Not one to miss an opportunity, she decided it was a perfect time to play "Princess." She pulled her stepping stool into my bathroom and proceeded to help herself to my cosmetics.

By the time the boys got back to the scene of the

threatened pounding, most of the antagonists had left. The few who remained seemed more interested in organizing a game of touch football than visiting bodily harm on a fourth grader. My sons decided to stick around and play defense.

I turned toward home, thankful no violence had occurred. Then I remembered the pot of spaghetti sauce I had set on the burner just before the boys came in from school. Running the two blocks back to the house, I burst in the front door and raced to the kitchen. The sauce bubbled merrily like a small volcano spewing tomato lava over the range top and floor. I clapped a lid on the pot and turned down the heat before tossing my coat over a chair and starting the kitchen clean-up. I was on my knees, scrubbing spaghetti sauce out of the grout when my daughter strolled into the room.

"Look, Mommy, I'm a princess!" she announced, twirling dramatically.

I sat back on my heels and gasped. She had draped a lace tablecloth over her head and it trailed behind her like a Viennese wedding veil. Dressed in an old half-slip and a pair of my high-heeled pumps she was adorned with the contents of my jewelry box. A half-inch of "Sparkling Burgundy" lipstick outlined her smile and her eyes sparkled beneath brows and eyelids weighted with blue eyeliner. Rounding out the vision were two asymmetrical circles of rouge. Her hands were covered with lipstick and eyeliner. As she took a step toward me, her heel caught in the tablecloth. She reached up to steady herself on the refrigerator, creating a brilliant freestyle design in red and blue.

"Stop!" I commanded. "Don't move!" Grabbing her, I pulled the "veil" from her hair and marched her upstairs to my room. My makeup was in disarray, my lingerie was strewn on the floor, and there were shoes all over the bottom of the closet. I scolded her for getting into my things and ran a tub of warm water. By the time she was scrubbed clean she was in repentant tears. After she was dried off and dressed, I set her to work putting my clothes away while I cleaned up and salvaged what was left of my makeup.

When we finished, we trudged down to the kitchen to start on the fridge just as the boys burst in from their flag football game. Laughing and pushing one another, they smeared clumps of muddy grass across the floor grinding the rich black earth into the newly cleaned grout.

"Just stop! Everyone stop!" I yelled. Instantly three pairs of eyes fixed on mine. A heavy silence filled the room as I took in the mess.

"Mommy's not feeling very happy today!" my daughter offered in explanation.

"She certainly isn't!" I added.

The next hour was spent cleaning up and listening to the latest installment in my week-long lecture series on responsibility and helpfulness. None of us felt much better when the evening ended and we fell into our beds.

At breakfast the next morning, I looked at the glum faces of my three children and made a decision. "Let's write down everything that went wrong this past week." I suggested. I'm sure they thought this list would become more fuel for the fires of my righteous indignation, but I had another plan. When we exhausted our memories, we had more than two dozen items on our list. Taking the paper, I placed it in a pie plate and lit the corner with a match. The kids watched with fascination as the flames licked at the words, curling the paper into black ashes until the list was consumed.

"Now," I said with finality. "That was last week. It's over and done and past. Let's just forget it and start all over with a fresh new week."

The relief on the faces of my children made me smile. We hugged and I ruffled their hair as they grabbed their lunches and headed for the school bus stop. I watched them until they turned the corner and were out of sight, then whispered a prayer. "Thank You, Lord, for another chance to do things better."

Reflections

There are times when we all need a fresh start. Mothers, fathers, children all say and do things we wish we hadn't. We burst out judgments in anger. We act thoughtlessly and cause others pain or worry. We do the right thing, but in the wrong way. Sometimes we're just plain ornery! These are the times when it is good to recall we have a Savior who delights in offering us an opportunity to start fresh once more.

The apostle John told of an incident where Jesus dramatically demonstrated this. Jesus had been in the temple courts in Jerusalem since dawn. Crowds gathered to listen and learn about the kingdom of God. As He sat teaching them, the sound of angry voices could be heard. The crowd parted as a group of robed lawyers and Pharisees pushed their way to the front. Two of the bearded scholars held a weeping woman by her arms, half dragging her along. When they were just a few feet in front of Jesus, they pushed the woman forward. One of them cleared his throat and drew his robes around himself with dignity. He raised an accusatory finger, pointing at the woman who stood now with her head bowed, alone.

"Teacher, this woman was caught in the act of adultery. In the Law Moses commanded us to stone such women. Now what do You say?" They were using this question as a trap, in order to have a basis for accusing Him.

But Jesus bent down and started to write on the ground with His finger. When they kept on questioning Him, He straightened up and said to them, "If any one of you is without sin, let him be the first to throw a stone at her." Again He stooped down and wrote on the ground.

> *At this, those who heard began to go away one at a time, the older ones first, until only Jesus was left, with the woman still standing there. Jesus straightened up and asked her, "Woman, where are they? Has no one condemned you?"*
>
> *"No one, sir," she said.*
>
> *"Then neither do I condemn you," Jesus declared. "Go now and leave your life of sin." John 8:4–11*

There was no doubt that the woman was guilty. She didn't deny it and Jesus acknowledged her "life of sin." What is remarkable about this incident is the way Jesus invites all the participants to leave their past way of living and start over. Without condemning the self-righteous Pharisees, he encourages them to abandon their judgmental attitudes. He appeals to the lawyers to rethink their interpretation of the Law. And He commands the sinful woman to forsake her former lifestyle. Everyone there that day had an opportunity to start over, to begin fresh once more.

It is inevitable that living in families, we irritate one another at times. It is easy to respond in ways that hurt feelings and foster bitterness. Sometimes it's tempting to carry a grudge, to make another pay for our hurt or refuse to ask for or grant forgiveness. These are the times we need to drop our stones of resentment and be willing to start fresh. Giving one another the opportunity to begin again with a clean slate not only fosters family harmony, it brings the example of Christlike love into our homes.

Scripture for Further Meditation

Get rid of all bitterness, rage and anger, brawling and slander, along with every form of malice. Be kind and compassionate to one another, forgiving each other, just as in Christ God forgave you. Ephesians 4:31–32

Practical Application

Consider whether you have been holding a grudge or resentment against someone in your family. Prayerfully ask God to remove that feeling from your heart and to give you His peace and love in its place. Write a note or speak to the other person, suggesting the two of you start fresh in your relationship. Refuse to refer to past hurts or bring up old issues again, trusting God to help you model His forgiving and restoring love.

Prayer

Lord, I know that You continually allow me to start over when I bring my past failures to You. I thank You that You offer me an opportunity to begin fresh with each new day and that in Your strength I can break old patterns of thought or action. Help me to offer others that same opportunity and to demonstrate Your love to those around me. Amen.

That's Not Fair!

AFTER THREE YEARS IN HAWAII, we moved to the Pacific Northwest and our daughter couldn't wait to experience the seasons. Fall came with its splendor, drenching our yard in red and golden leaves. We planted tulip and daffodil bulbs in the garden beds, anticipating their springtime glory. And when the first frost arrived, Anne was sure the long-awaited winter couldn't be far behind.

One November afternoon she dashed in from school waving a sheaf of papers. "Ski Club!" she squealed with adolescent delight. "Can you believe they actually take you up to the mountains for skiing every week? Can I go? Please?"

We read through all the paperwork and decided it would be a wonderful opportunity for her. Scouting through secondhand stores, we accumulated the appropriate ski clothing and equipment. Her Christmas money helped pay the transportation and lesson costs and she eagerly awaited the first class to be held in early January.

On the Friday morning of the first ski trip, she packed her bags with skis, boots, poles, and enough dinner for two hungry hikers. We dropped her off at school early so she could deposit all her gear in the ski shack. Half an hour after school, the bus would pick up the skiers and head for the slopes. We were to pick our students up at 11:00 P.M. when the bus returned. All day long I thought about her long-await-ed adventure, hoping reality would meet her very high expectations. I watched the ski report on the television and learned there were 10 inches of new powder in the mountains—near perfect conditions.

At 11:00 I waited with other parents as the steamy charter bus rolled into the school parking lot. The sponsoring teacher got off the bus and gathered the waiting parents for an announcement. The kids had enjoyed a great trip and no one was hurt, she told us, but on the way home someone was horsing around and threw a penny, striking the bus driver in the head. While he wasn't hurt, the teacher felt he could have been distracted and might have swerved, caus-ing an accident. It was a safety issue and if the stu-dents involved didn't come forward and confess, she was canceling the following week's trip. She expressed hope that we would support her in this decision.

The children leaving the bus were subdued as they gathered their equipment and headed for their cars. I spotted Anne's parka as she worked her way down the bus aisle. Helping her locate her skis and bag, I asked how things went.

"It was so fantastic!" she bubbled. "The snow was

beautiful and I had so much fun. The instructor said I was doing really well with my wedge and I learned how to climb up a hill with skis on and how to turn. It was just awesome!"

As we shoved her equipment into the van and climbed in, her mood changed. "But did you hear what happened? It's just so unfair. The teacher may cancel the next trip because some of the boys were horsing around and threw a penny and it hit the driver! I can't believe it. I mean nobody got hurt. It was stupid, but why do we all have to be punished? If I don't get to go next week, I'll be a week behind on my lessons and we paid for seven weeks and now we only get six! It's not fair!"

I had to admit, it didn't seem fair, but I could also see the teacher's side. What if the bus had swerved on an icy road and the kids had been injured? All of them would have been involved in an accident because of the actions of a few and that wouldn't have been fair either.

I suggested we leave things up to the teacher and the administration and pray that the parties involved would come forward. She agreed that was about all we could do, but remained unconvinced that anyone would own up to the misbehavior. I wasn't hopeful either. All we could do was wait for Wednesday when the final decision would be made.

Monday, the schools were closed due to a snow-storm. On Tuesday, the ski club instructor was out of the building all day and tension was building among the young skiers. Wednesday morning they announced that those responsible for the incident on the bus had come forward. They would be suspended from the ski trip that week, but everyone else could go.

When I picked up my daughter after school, she was ebullient. "Isn't it great how God answered our prayers and everything worked out? He's so good!" she exclaimed.

I agreed it was, but then I posed a question. "Anne, suppose the kids hadn't come forward and the ski trip had been canceled. Would God still be good?"

She looked at me with a puzzled expression as she wrestled with the question. I knew her struggle. It's easy to proclaim God's love and goodness when things work out the way we want. But life doesn't always work out that way. And when our dreams are unfulfilled, or our hopes shattered, when we suffer injustice, how is our perception of God affected?

Reflections

While youngsters frequently complain they receive unfair treatment, fairness is a tough issue. Why is it that some of us prosper while others can't seem to get ahead? When a tornado or brush fire sweeps through a neighborhood, why are some homes untouched? Why do innocents suffer and criminals escape punishment? The world is filled with inequities and our hearts cry out that it's just not fair.

Some people assume God must not care about those treated unfairly, but I believe Scripture reveals a picture of a very concerned heavenly Father.

In the last 14 chapters of Genesis we read the account of Joseph, a man who was treated unfairly by just about everyone he knew. The youngest of 11 brothers, Joseph was favored by his father, Jacob, which bred jealousy in the hearts of Jacob's other sons. When Joseph came to them in the desert with food and messages from his father, they stripped him, threw him into a pit, and eventually sold him as a slave to a passing caravan headed for Egypt. Purchased by Potifar, a wealthy Egyptian official, Joseph worked diligently until Potifar's wife falsely accused him of rape after he refused her seductive advances. Unfairly imprisoned, he served the warden with such integrity that he gained authority over the other prisoners. When Joseph interpreted a dream spelling freedom for an imprisoned royal baker, he was promised an early release. But once freed, the baker forgot his promise and Joseph languished in prison two additional years. How unfair!

Through a divinely orchestrated series of events, Joseph eventually rose to a position of authority in Egypt second only to that of Pharaoh. Then he had an opportunity for revenge. His starving brothers came to him seeking food and Joseph had to decide how to repay them for their unfairness. Through several tests Joseph evaluated the integrity of his former tormentors and decided on a course of action.

Exercising forgiveness and mercy, he provided for their survival and prosperity. When they finally recognized him as the brother they wronged, they questioned his unexpected response. Joseph replied: " 'Don't be afraid. Am I in the place of God? You intended to harm me, but God intended it for good to accomplish what is now being done, the saving of many lives. So then, don't be afraid. I will provide for you and your children.' And he reassured them and spoke kindly to them." Genesis 50:19–21

It would have been easy for Joseph to make his brothers pay for treating him unfairly. But he learned an important lesson during years of mistreatment. He realized only God sees the whole picture of our lives. What seems unfair to us may, from God's perspective, be what benefits not only us but those around us as well. It is easy to forget our perspective is not the only one to consider. When I am tempted to seek self-justification or retribution from those I believe have treated me unfairly, I need to prayerfully consider Joseph's words. Could it be God has a good plan at work?

Scripture for Further Meditation

And we know that in all things God works for the good of those who love Him, who have been called according to His purpose. Romans 8:28

Practical Application

Read through the story of Joseph in Genesis 37–50. As you read, note the verses where God's hand is evident in Joseph's life. (For example, Genesis 39:2—"The Lord was with Joseph and he prospered.") Think about times you have felt unfairly treated. Prayerfully ask God to show you evidence of His hand in and through those circumstances. When you are tempted to seek retribution, recall Joseph's words to his brothers. Ask God for wisdom in your own response.

Prayer

Dear Lord, I live in a world that is often unfair. My human response is to lash out in indignation, but I know that seldom results in Your righteousness. Give me a heart to see beyond my own wisdom to Your plan. Help me have faith in Your ability to bring about good from the unfairness I see. Let me be a part of the healing process, not a party to further hurt. Amen.

Me First!

It was the morning of our son's sixth birthday. He jumped out of bed without coaxing and wolfed down his breakfast with relish. "How long until my party, Mom?" he asked, stuffing the last bite of toast into his mouth.

I glanced at the clock. "Six hours, Doug. The party isn't until 2:00 this afternoon."

He sighed. I smiled and offered him more toast. "Tell you what. You can help me decorate and get the games ready and the time will go by quickly."

Together we taped crepe paper streamers along the walls in the dining room. We tacked an old sheet across the hall doorway as a "fish pond" where his guests could dangle a paper clip hook from a bamboo pole as they fished for a prize. He was crazy about G.I. Joe that year, so we set up the "Pin the Wings on the Bomber" game in the family room and hid dozens of cheap plastic army men in the backyard for the "Spy Hunt." He could hardly stand still as we blew up balloons and hung the Birthday Flag from the pole on the front porch.

When I started to frost the cake—angelfood with

camouflage frosting per his request—he suggested we decorate it with tiny army planes and artistically "crashed" several into the top and sides. It was a sight to behold.

At 1:50 P.M., he stationed himself on the front walk to await his guests. Eight little boys finally arrived, each one almost as excited as our son. They tumbled into the house, laughing and shouting, batting at the balloons and leaping to touch the swaying streamers.

"How about some games?" I suggested, hoping to focus their unbridled energy.

"Yeah!" they chorused, clustering around me expectantly.

"I'll go first," shouted my son, dashing to the fishing game. "I get to be first because I'm the birthday boy!"

It had never occurred to me he would demand to be first. I quickly intervened. "No, Doug, our guests go first." I lined up the boys and handed the fishing pole to a freckle-faced redhead who caught a plastic whistle. When everyone had a turn at fishing, we moved to "Pin the Wings on the Bomber."

"Me first!" my son insisted. "Birthday boy goes first!" Again I interrupted and reminded him as host, he should be last. He unsuccessfully vied for first place in the remaining games. By the time we got to the refreshments, he was frustrated and close to tears.

The cake, with its dollops of green and brown

frosting, was a big hit. The opening of gifts was a frenzy of ribbon and paper punctuated with shouts of delight. The boys enjoyed themselves and left happily clutching their prizes and plastic army men. Only my little birthday boy looked a bit glum when the last guest departed.

"What a great party!" I observed as we walked back into the house.

"Yeah, but it would have been even better if I got to be first in the games. Mom, everybody knows the birthday boy gets to be first. It's your special day."

"I can't believe you're so worried about being first," I exclaimed. "You had a wonderful party with great friends and received beautiful gifts. You're upset because you didn't get to be first? You don't have to always be the center of attention, you know." I shook my head at him.

His shoulders slumped and I watched as he gathered up his birthday presents and took them to his room. All the morning's joy evaporated.

As I cleaned up the dining room I thought how sad it was that my son's reluctance to allow others to go first had marred his excitement. Rather than treating his friends in a special way, he demanded that honor for himself. He was certainly old enough to know better. I was tempted to treat him to one of my parental lectures, when a scene from just a few days earlier flashed through my mind.

I was driving home from a PTA meeting in a foul mood because someone had taken my idea for a fund raiser, given it a catchy title, presented it to the board, and been hailed as a creative whiz. Never once had she acknowledged that the suggestion was originally mine. I was stung by her insensitivity and jealous of the attention she received—attention I felt I deserved. Now it all seemed very petty—and very similar to my 6-year-old son's behavior. I licked a smudge of chocolate frosting off my thumb and looked around the room at the remnants of the party. How like my son I was—missing out on the abundant joy around me while I selfishly proclaimed, "Me first!"

Reflections

Insisting on our rights, demanding recognition, striving to be acclaimed as first or best are natural inclinations. Western society encourages this bent toward self-elevation and while we often praise the humble, none of us is too anxious to join their ranks. In God's kingdom, however, there is a different guiding principle at work. Time and again Jesus reminds His followers the first will be last and those seeking to be elevated first must learn to have the heart of a slave.

About 2,000 years ago there was a power struggle between the followers of two itinerant teachers. There were several similarities between them: they were both poor, neither had been formally educated, they each rose from obscurity and attracted a group of devoted followers. Their messages were similar as well, urging men and women to turn their hearts to God. The Bible tells us they were even related. The older of the two, John began his ministry much earlier than Jesus. Yet when Jesus entered the scene, John announced his unlimited support and devotion to Him. During the months that followed, John's disciples grew defensive. This upstart, Jesus, was stealing away all their converts. People were flocking to Him to be baptized! One can almost hear their wails, "But we were here first!"

They came to John and said to him, "Rabbi, that man who was with you on the other side of the Jordan—the one you testified about—well, He is baptizing, and everyone is going to Him."

To this John replied, "A man can receive only what is given him from heaven. You yourselves can testify that I said, 'I am not the Christ but am sent ahead of Him.' The bride belongs to the bridegroom. The friend who attends the bridegroom waits and listens for him, and is full of joy when he hears the bridegroom's voice. That joy is mine, and it is now complete. He must become greater; I must become less." John 3:26–30

John exemplified the opposite of the "me-first" attitude that many of us share. It didn't bother him that Jesus was more popular or received more credit. And I think the key to his attitude was the understanding expressed in this passage, "A man can receive only what is given him from heaven." God determines the place each one deserves.

John continued with his ministry even though Jesus attracted more followers. He even continued when he was unjustly arrested and imprisoned for offending the selfish, self-promoting wife of Herod the Tetrarch. And when Jesus learned of John's humiliation He turned to His own followers and said, "I tell you the truth: Among those born of women there has not risen anyone greater than John the Baptist" (Matthew 11:11).

God knows the plans He has for each of us. There are times we will be elevated and times we will be brought low. My job is to do the task set before me and let the Lord worry about who gets the credit. When I become obsessed about being noticed, about being first, I end up like my son—losing the joy God intended for me.

Scripture for Further Meditation

Do nothing out of selfish ambition or vain conceit, but in humility consider others better than yourselves.
Philippians 2:3

Practical Application

Make it a practice to encourage your family and friends. Express appreciation for their help and give them credit for their contributions. Write notes of encouragement to those in leadership in your church or community, being specific about how their leadership has positively affected you. When you are involved in a project at home, church, or in the community, seek to do it for the Lord's pleasure, not for the praise or thanks of others.

Prayer

Dear Lord, I find it so easy to become self-centered. Forgive me for the times I push myself forward, demanding credit and desiring recognition. Help me be content knowing I am special to You. Give me an attitude of humility, seeking to express my appreciation and love for others. Thank You for affirming my worth to You through the enduring love of Jesus Christ. Amen.

But What Will My Friends Say?

WE MOVED TO ALEXANDRIA, VIRGINIA, when our second son was just entering junior high. He was a good student and enjoyed sports, but most of the kids in his class were old friends and, as the newcomer, he had a tough time breaking into the social structure. It was several months before a small group of friends called regularly, came over, and invited him to participate in an impromptu game of baseball or football.

I didn't realize how much he counted on this little group until one day in December when I grabbed his backpack to stick in some extra notebook paper he asked me to buy. There were three clean shirts stuffed in the bag.

"What's this?" I asked, pulling out the shirts.

My son looked up from his breakfast. "Oh, those are my extra shirts in case I need a different one after I get to school."

Still puzzled, I continued, "Why would you need a different one?"

He sighed as only teenagers can. "You wouldn't understand."

"Try me."

"OK. Let's say I get to school and Chris has on a shirt like the one I'm wearing. I don't want him to think I copied him, so I change. Or if everyone has on a T-shirt and I wore a collared one, I can take it off and put on a T-shirt. I just don't want to be a geek, Mom."

"I don't get it. Why can't they all change and you be the one with the right shirt on?"

"See, I told you you wouldn't understand. They're popular. I'm not. It's just the way things work."

How do you fight the impeccable logic of adolescence? He left for school with his shirt wardrobe intact.

A few weeks later I was delighted to receive a notice in the mail announcing our son had been selected to join the Junior Honor Society. The application for membership and invitation to the induction ceremony were included. I couldn't wait to share the good news with him!

"Look!" I called, waving the invitation at him when he came home from school. "Isn't this wonderful? We're so proud of you!"

He read the letter and slumped into the chair. "Oh, this is just great. There's no way I'm going to join the Junior Honor Society." The last three words were spoken with disgust.

"Why not?" I inquired.

"You wouldn't understand, Mom."

"Try me."

"None of my friends are in the Junior Honor Society. It's a stupid bunch of geeky kids nobody likes and I'm not joining. What would all my friends say? It's taken too long to get them to accept me anyway and I'm not going to risk losing them now." He picked up his backpack and headed for his room.

"You're right." I called after him. "I don't get it." But I held my tongue.

Later, when his dad and I discussed it with him, he was just as firm. Our adult reasoning fell on deaf ears. The reality of our world, where membership in the Honor Society was admired, didn't matter. In his world of emerging macho maleness, the Honor Society was the kiss of death.

In the end he didn't join.

For a while I wondered where we went wrong. Did he have so little confidence that his identity was only defined by others? Why couldn't he stand up and be the trendsetter? Why did he care so much about the opinions of a few pimply boys? And then I recalled my reluctance just days earlier to speak up about an issue at a school meeting because I feared the disapproval of others. Despite being a "grown-up" I could hear my son's words echo in my own thoughts: "What would all my friends say?"

Reflections

Most of us are concerned to some extent about what our friends think. We're afraid how they might react if we do or say the wrong thing. We might lose our position or prestige. We might be labeled *troublemaker* if we question the status quo, or *fanatic* if we speak up about a moral issue. Enslaved by such fears many of us refuse to defend our faith when it is attacked. We go along with a group when we may not even agree with it. We sit safely in our church pew instead of stepping out onto the battlefield of the world.

This is not a new phenomenon. Back in the first century there were lots of cowards too. In John 9 we read the story of a man who was blind from birth. He was relegated to a life of poverty, begging in the streets. One day Jesus passed by this poor man and healed him. It was a miracle and everyone in the town knew about it. The ever-vigilant Pharisees decided to get to the bottom of the blind man's story so they questioned his neighbors and friends. After several inquiries, they asked the man's parents about the healing. Listen to their response and the commentary provided by John:

"We know he is our son," the parents answered, "and we know he was born blind. But how he can see now, or who opened his eyes, we don't know. Ask him. He is of age; he will speak for himself."

> *His parents said this because they were afraid of the Jews, for already the Jews had decided that anyone who acknowledged that Jesus was the Christ would be put out of the synagogue. That was why his parents said, "He is of age; ask him." John 9:20–23*

These poor parents were paralyzed by their fear. What if they lost their place in the synagogue? What would the neighbors think? How would it affect business? Better to stay timid, quiet, and safe.

It is easy to understand these folks. After all, they really didn't know much about this Jesus fellow. He just strolled into town one day and healed their son. Surely if they had spent time with Him, they would have been more willing to speak of their faith in Him. Not necessarily. On the night He was betrayed, Jesus and His disciples were in the garden of Gethsemane when a mob led by Judas and his pals from the local synagogue arrived. After identifying his Master with a betraying kiss, Judas stepped back to let his companions seize Christ. As they began to haul Jesus away, "all the disciples deserted Him and fled" (Matthew 26:56).

It is clear they were terrified, imagining what might happen to them if they claimed to be followers of Jesus. Despite living and ministering with their Master for three years, they were still afraid to risk their reputations and their lives for Him.

Whether we are newly acquainted with Christ or have been walking with Him for a while, many of us struggle with fear when the opportunity comes to defend our faith. What will happen to us? What will our friends and family think? Will our comfortable world be upset? Fear grips us and we remain silent, unwilling to risk criticism or disapproval.

On our own, we often discover we lack the courage of our convictions. But God has not left us on our own. He reveals in His Word the source of unlimited courage—the Holy Spirit, available to us through our Savior, Jesus Christ.

Filled with the Spirit, the once timid disciples boldly proclaimed their faith before thousands gathered in Jerusalem for Pentecost. Throughout Luke's Acts of the Apostles, we see the courage and faith of these and other followers of Christ. Men and women who formerly hid in the shadows now risked their lives, not caring what others thought. What is the source of their newfound courage? The same Holy Spirit, poured out on the disciples in fulfillment of Christ's promise recorded in John 16.

When Paul wrote to Timothy, a young man who struggled with teaching the truth to those who thought they already knew it all, he encouraged him with these words about the Holy Spirit: "For God did not give us a spirit of timidity, but a spirit of power, of love and of self-discipline" (2 Timothy 1:7).

These same words are the key to overcoming our fears. In His loving kindness, God provides us with courage through His Holy Spirit who lives in all believers. When I am afraid, I call upon His boldness to speak or to take a stand. When I prayerfully seek His wisdom and understanding, He promises to direct my actions and words. And if others misunderstand or oppose me, He is my comfort. There are no promises in Scripture that we can escape frightening situations, but we do have wonderful promises that Jesus will enable us to overcome our fears.

Scripture for Further Meditation

But you will receive power when the Holy Spirit comes on you; and you will be my witnesses in Jerusalem, and in all Judea and Samaria, and to the ends of the earth. Acts 1:8

Practical Application

Ask God to make you sensitive to opportunities to speak up for Him. Determine to depend upon the Holy Spirit for courage when the moment arrives. The next time you are in a situation where your faith is challenged, politely but firmly declare your reasons for believing as you do. If you have time to prepare your comments, jot down your main ideas and search the Scriptures for additional insights. Speaking up in defense of your beliefs is a faith-strengthening exercise.

Prayer

Dear Jesus, I confess it is often tempting to care more about the opinions of others than what You think. Forgive me when I allow my fear of disapproval to keep me silent. Grant me the courage to speak for You with clarity and truth inspired by the wisdom of Your Holy Spirit. Thank You for Your enabling power. Amen.

I'm Sorry

WHEN OUR SONS WERE 8 AND 4, I gave birth to a daughter. We were delighted to add a girl to our family but I wondered if she would develop into a tomboy, following after two older brothers. Anyone with children knows they come equipped with their own agendas and it wasn't long before hers became evident.

From the time she could crawl our daughter was attracted by things one might consider feminine. She preferred dolls to trucks, playing house to playing war, and pink to any other color in the spectrum. Her temperament, though strong-willed, showed a sensitivity to others that could quickly fill her eyes with sympathetic tears.

From her earliest days she performed little kindnesses for all of us—whether we desired them or not! She left playdough cookies by the bedside where my husband stepped on them with a bare foot. She lovingly bathed the cat with half a bottle of shampoo. She added a paragraph or two of asterisks to a manuscript I left in the electric typewriter and mailed a handful of important letters for us by placing them in the litter container on the corner. It was difficult to be angry with her because she was usually well-intentioned and when confronted with wrong-doing, was immediately and sincerely repentant.

The boys teased her about being "little miss perfect" but she really wasn't. She just possessed a genuinely sweet spirit and received joy from making others happy. When friends commented on her good nature, I laughed and remarked that God, in His mercy, knew I would be in my 50s when she was a teenager and must have decided to give me an easy time of it!

One night, when our daughter was about 8, I awoke around midnight to find her standing at the foot of our bed. At first I thought I was dreaming. "Anne?" I whispered. "Is something wrong?"

She nodded and walked around to my side of the bed. "I really need to tell you something, Mommy," she said softly.

I swung my legs over the side of the bed and slid my feet into my slippers. Putting my finger to my lips and pointing to my sleeping husband, I took her hand and we tiptoed out to the family room. I flipped on a small lamp near the couch and sat, pulling her down beside me.

"Are you sick, honey?" I inquired, placing my hand on her forehead.

She shook her head and studied the edge of her pajama top, fiddling nervously with a bit of lace. "I did something bad and I kept it a secret and now I can't sleep and I need to tell you." She glanced up quickly to check my reaction to her announcement.

I couldn't imagine what could produce this kind of guilt. I was sure it wasn't anything too serious, but obviously she felt otherwise. "You know you can tell me anything, Anne."

She sighed. "And you will still love me just as much, right?"

I tucked my arm around her and held her close. "Always and always. There is nothing you could say that would make me stop loving you."

Taking a deep breath, she embarked on a tale of how several days earlier she had been playing Princess with her friends in the backyard and had "borrowed" some of my costume jewelry to enhance their wardrobes. After everyone left and she was returning the jewelry, she found one of the pins was damaged and hid it in her room so I wouldn't find out.

"But I knew it was there, Mommy, and every time I looked at it I just felt worse. And I didn't want you to be mad, but I ..." she opened her hand and held out the offending article.

It was a silver pin shaped like a bow. Once shiny, it was now bent and scratched. It looked like it had been scraped along the sidewalk. I took the pin from her and turned it over in my hand.

"I'm so sorry. I could pay you back for it. I have some money in my bank." She looked at me hopefully, her eyes shiny behind a layer of tears.

"Well, I think we can work something out," I said. "But the most important thing is that you remember how this happened. You took something without asking. You damaged it and then you tried to hide the truth. And then you felt bad about it for days. I'm really glad you told me about it. I love you and I forgive you. I know you have learned some very important lessons about being honest from this whole thing."

She cried then, soaking my nightgown with tears as she hugged me. Her relief was palpable. I stroked her hair and wondered at the power of guilt and forgiveness. When we wrong someone we love, it brings a pain that burns. The forgiveness of that loved one soothes like cooling waters.

When she was calm once more and I had tucked her back into her bed, I returned to my room. In the moonlight I examined the ruined silver pin. Instead of tossing it in the trash, I decided to tuck it into a corner of my drawer. Its dulled reflection would serve as a reminder of the night my daughter and I shared a moment of deep truth.

Reflections

It's easy to excuse ourselves as we stomp through life, treading carelessly over others' possessions and personalities. Many of us are insensitive to the damage and hurt we cause. Unkind remarks, irresponsible behavior, and withheld kindness build barriers of resentment and guilt. Then we wonder why we have a feeling of general malaise or bouts of depression. Although there are certainly medical reasons for some of this, I suspect many of us could experience great relief by seeking forgiveness from God and others. There is a cleansing in forgiveness that lifts the soul and spirit as well as the mind and body.

This is not a new idea, nor is it one springing from pop psychology. The Bible speaks of the power of forgiveness in countless passages, and perhaps never with such beauty as in the actions of a young woman who found the freedom of forgiveness at the feet of Jesus.

It was a warm Gallilean night and Jesus had been invited to eat dinner with Simon, a wealthy Pharisee. Ushered into the home of his host, Jesus took His place and reclined at the table as was the custom. Soon, the Pharisee and his other guests were deep in conversation with the Teacher, no doubt discussing His views on the religious Law. And then, something quite unprecedented occurred.

When a woman who had lived a sinful life in that town learned that Jesus was eating at the Pharisee's house, she brought an alabaster jar of perfume, and as she stood behind Him at His feet weeping, she began to wet His feet with her tears. Then she wiped them with her hair, kissed them and poured perfume on them.

> *When the Pharisee who had invited Him saw this, he said to himself, "If this man were a prophet, He would know who is touching Him and what kind of woman she is—that she is a sinner."*
>
> *Jesus answered him, "Simon, I have something to tell you."*
>
> *"Tell me, Teacher," he said.*
>
> *"Two men owed money to a certain moneylender. One owed him five hundred denarii, and the other fifty. Neither of them had the money to pay him back, so he canceled the debts of both. Now which of them will love him more?"*
>
> *Simon replied, "I suppose the one who had the bigger debt canceled."*
>
> *"You have judged correctly," Jesus said.* Luke 7:37–43

As Jesus continued to instruct Simon, the woman continued to minister to her Savior until Jesus lovingly turned to her and said, "Therefore, I tell you, her many sins have been forgiven—for she loved much. But he who has been forgiven little loves little" (Luke 7:47).

I suspect this woman went away from that evening completely changed. Her heart was lightened, not only because she had emptied it of her guilt and darkness, but also because it was filled with Christ's love and purity. She could have remained as she was, burdened by her sin, weighed down with the resentment of others, and excluded from the blessings of forgiveness. But she chose instead to risk trusting her life to God's love, which poured into her and set her free.

When my daughter came to me with her guilty confession, she expressed her trust in our love for each other. Likewise, when I go to God with my sin and guilt, I cast myself upon His love expressed to me through Jesus Christ. And He promises not only to forgive, but also to restore my joy, replacing my unhealthy darkness with His healing light.

Scripture for Further Meditation

If we confess our sins, He is faithful and just and will forgive us our sins and purify us from all unrighteousness. 1 John 1:9

Practical Application

Spend some time in prayer examining your relationships with God and others. Claiming the promise of God in 1 John 1:9, specifically name sins that are troubling you, and ask God's forgiveness. If there are those you have harmed with words, actions, or attitudes of resentment, seek their forgiveness as well. It may be difficult for you but the freedom and cleansing is well worth any discomfort you may experience. (Remember, the response of others is their responsibility. Yours is to humbly seek forgiveness where you have caused offense.)

Prayer

Dear Father, I know I have sinned against You and against others. I confess these things to You now. I long to know the lifting of my guilt and the freedom of Your forgiveness. Thank You for the promise of Your cleansing love offered to me through Your Son, Jesus Christ. Amen.

Somebody's Watching

FOR 28 YEARS MY HUSBAND WAS AN OFFICER in the United States Navy. This gave our family many opportunities to experience new cultures and new friends as well as an abundance of challenges like moving and changing and adjusting. As our three children grew, we frequently reminded them how fortunate they were to be able to live in interesting places and see and do special things. We also reminded them they were being watched, not by us necessarily, but by others who worked for their father. People were interested to see how the boss' kids acted, and their interest wasn't always benevolent. We weren't sure if the children believed what we told them—until our second son experienced it firsthand.

My husband called from work to tell me he had an interesting message from one of his superior officers at the Navy's Pacific Fleet Headquarters at Pearl Harbor. According to the message, our 17-year-old son had a minor run-in with Base Security the night before. The French Ambassador and his wife were in town for ceremonies scheduled to commemorate the

50th anniversary of the end of World War II. As their chauffeured car pulled up to the official guest cottage provided by the Navy, the Ambassador's wife was upset to find three teenaged boys lounging on her patio! Her exposure to American teens apparently came from Hollywood and she questioned the security surrounding her visit.

Security officers arrived and ascertained that the boys lived nearby, were all sons of senior officers, and were engaged in a conversation in the comfort of the guest house porch swing. The boys eagerly departed after begging the pardon of Mrs. French Ambassador.

The tone of the message was humorous and sent as a friendly ribbing to my husband but we agreed it might make an interesting topic for dinner conversation. Knowing our son obviously meant to keep this little incident a secret, we thought we could have some good-humored fun at his expense.

As we sat down to dinner my husband asked if anything interesting had gone on that day. Our daughter chattered on about happenings at her school. When she ran out of information I asked our son about his day. He mentioned a math test that had gone well and a new offensive play the football coach was working on.

"Have some more *French* fries?" my husband inquired, passing the potatoes.

"No," I responded, "but would you pass the *French* dressing?"

"It's right over there behind the *French*-cut green beans," he replied.

"Hey," our daughter interrupted. "That is so weird! Do you guys realize everything you mentioned has French in it?"

"How about that!" I said. "I guess there's just more French stuff around than anyone realizes. Wouldn't you say so, Doug?" We all looked at him expectantly as a pink flush crept up his face.

He finished his mouthful of food and swallowed slowly. He had the look of a cornered deer. "Oh man, how did you find out? It was really no big deal. Really. We weren't doing anything wrong."

My husband's cheek began to twitch as he struggled to suppress a smile. The smile won and Doug sighed with relief.

"I thought you were really mad at me, Dad!"

"No, it really wasn't such a big deal, but you can't expect us to pass up such a wonderful opportunity to give you a bad time can you?" He laughed and gave Doug a playful punch in the arm.

"Well, isn't anyone going to tell me what's going on?" interrupted Anne.

Doug launched into an entertaining description of his run-in with international politics and we all enjoyed his interpretation of the events, but when he finished he turned back to his dad.

"So how did you find out?" he asked.

My husband explained the message and then spent a few minutes reiterating the fact that we were all of interest to others around the base. It was not because we were any more important than others, but that his position as Commanding Officer created curiosity. Some people wondered if we lived up to their expectations. Others were hoping we wouldn't. Whatever the reason, he concluded, somebody is watching you, so watch yourself!

The incident of the "French Ambassador's Wife" has taken its place among all the other bits and pieces of family lore, but it always reminds me of an important truth. As a child of my heavenly Father, I realize others are watching me. Because of this I need to remember to watch myself as well.

Reflections

We live in a country where individualism and self-reliance are guiding principles, so it is easy to forget our lives are inextricably intertwined with others. We like to feel independent and often judge as mature those who act without regard to the opinions of others. But when we become citizens of Christ's kingdom, things often change.

Almost 2,000 years ago, there was an aristocrat from one of the finest families in Israel. Gifted with a brilliant mind and keen intellect, his parents sent him to study with Gamaliel, the best teacher of the Law in Jerusalem. After completing his education, fired with zeal and determination, this young man, Paul of

Tarsus, set out to destroy the enemies of God.

Under his direction families were dragged from their homes, beaten and imprisoned for professing faith in Jesus Christ. Paul cared nothing about what people thought. He ignored the opinions of those with whom he disagreed. His mission was clear. Guided by self-righteousness, convinced of his own faultless judgment, he cut a swath of death and destruction through the emerging Christian church.

Then Paul met Jesus. Struck down on the road to Damascus by the hand of God, the arrogant zealot who thought he knew everything, became blind and confused. After several days God's mercy and grace restored his vision and revealed the truth. Paul was a different man. From that moment on, he sought to convey what he had learned: that Jesus was the Christ, the Messiah, and had come to save sinners like Paul.

But something else was different about Paul as well. He realized he was no longer independent and self-reliant, operating in a vacuum. He had a new appreciation of his responsibility to demonstrate, through his everyday life, that he was his Father's child. Paul knew people were watching him. Some were hoping to see him revert to his old ways and discredit Christ. Others saw him as a model. Still others watched to learn more about what it meant to be a believer. The man who had cared little about the opinions of others now determined to live as a glowing and positive representative of God's love in the world. Listen to what he tells members of the church in Corinth as they struggle with this issue of their new-found freedom in Christ:

> *Be careful, however, that the exercise of your freedom does not become a stumbling block to the weak. 1 Corinthians 8:9*
>
> *When you sin against your brothers in this way and wound their weak conscience, you sin against Christ. Therefore, if what I eat causes my brother to fall into sin, I will never eat meat again, so that I will not cause him to fall. 1 Corinthians 8:12–13*
>
> *Though I am free and belong to no man, I make myself a slave to everyone, to win as many as possible. 1 Corinthians 9:19*
>
> *So whether you eat or drink or whatever you do, do it all for the glory of God. Do not cause anyone to stumble, whether Jews, Greeks or the church of God—even as I try to please everybody in every way. For I am not seeking my own good, but the good of many so that they may be saved. Follow my example, as I follow the example of Christ. 1 Corinthians 10:31–33*

These excerpts from Paul's lengthy discourse on the nature of our freedom in Christ state in eloquent terms the truth my husband and I tried to communicate to our children: Someone is watching you, so watch out!

As I go about my daily business as a wife, mother, employer, employee, volunteer, or citizen, I represent my Lord. Does my behavior cause others to stumble on their pathway of faith or does it encourage them to continue in the journey? My freedom in Christ is not a license to act independently of Him. People are watching me to learn more about my Father!

Scripture for Further Meditation

In the same way, let your light shine before men, that they may see your good deeds and praise your Father in heaven. Matthew 5:16

Practical Application

When considering what to wear, what to do, or what to say, take a moment to ask yourself how someone who is not a believer views you. Do your actions, words, and appearance reflect favorably on your Father in heaven? A good way to help your children, as well as yourself, is to submit decisions to the scrutiny of the question: What would Jesus do? Whether we like it or not, as believers, we are being watched. Understanding this can help us live the kind of life that encourages others to come to faith rather than reject it.

Prayer

Father, I realize that I often act as if You had no claim on me. In doing so I may weaken the faith of others. Forgive me please and make me ever mindful that I can be a reflection of Your love to those around me. Help me live in a way that brings glory to you. Amen.

Hey, Mom!

IT WAS A BALMY SUMMER DAY as we drove to the beach. Trade winds pushed puffy clouds across the sky and urged the ocean into perfect, white-crested waves. Arriving at the shore, the children took body boards, towels, and picnic gear down to the water's edge. They headed for the water, dashing into the warm surf with squeals of delight. I settled in my beach chair with a book, anticipating a few delicious hours of private time.

"Hey, Mom!" hollered my older son. "Watch me catch this one!"

I watched and signaled with an upraised thumb as he rode a perfectly curling wave all the way to the sandy shore. Readjusting my towel, I resumed reading. As I turned the page, a shadow fell over my shoulder. I looked up and my daughter stood beside me with her pail in hand.

"Hey, Mom, would you help me build a sand castle?" she asked, offering me her spare shovel.

I set my book aside and accompanied her to the site of her excavation. We dug and heaped and molded damp sand into ramparts and turrets. Then we decorated our structure with bits of shell and sea-weed she had scavenged from the shoreline. While we worked, she peppered me with questions about the ocean and how baby crabs find their mothers after they get dragged away from home by a wave. She discussed the beautiful mermaid who lived in her sandcastle and how a handsome prince would come from the sea to marry her. After awhile I returned to the solitude of my chair and book, lathering my sun-burned shoulders with another layer of lotion.

"Mom! Hey, Mom!" my younger son shouted as he ran up the beach toward me. "Hurry! Get the ten-derizer! I got stung by a jellyfish!"

I grabbed the jar of meat tenderizer we carried for just such emergencies and quickly mixed a spoonful with some fresh water. I gently dabbed the white paste over the tiny red bumps on my son's leg. The enzymes in the tenderizer soon neutralized the pain and after a generous dose of cookies and TLC, my son dashed back into the water.

Despite my determination to relax and read, I spent most of the afternoon admiring new body surf-ing techniques, critiquing interesting bits of flotsam, and doling out sunscreen and minor first aid. My children alternated between forgetting me entirely and wanting me desperately, coming and going as their needs dictated. In the end, after reading the same paragraph half a dozen times, I put my book down and watched my children as they played. I did-n't really resent their intrusions. It was reassuring to know they needed me, even if it was only on their terms at times. I smiled as I watched their strong young bodies shining in the sunlight, sparkling with sea foam and sand. My son turned, saw me watching him, grinned, and dove into a crashing wave.

And in that moment God gave me a glimpse of my relationship with Him. Each day He sends me out into the world. He grants me independence and freedom yet I am like my children, constantly returning to Him with questions and concerns, to share a delight, or ask for help. In His nearness I am given the courage to venture out, knowing He will be there when I call His name. And in our constant conversation, I experience the privilege and blessings of prayer.

Reflections

I used to think communing with God meant setting aside blocks of time to get alone with Him in what my Christian friends called a "private prayer closet." I tried to find such times and places, but my personal "prayer closet" seemed particularly cluttered and not very private. The demands of my life had a way of intruding. I sometimes felt guilty about this and often tried with renewed fervor to devote lengthy periods of time to prayer. I was never very successful.

What seemed to work better for me was catching

bits of time throughout the day. I sang praise songs to God in the car, meditated on His Word during baseball practice, had long conversations with Him while I ironed, vacuumed, and dusted. I shot arrow prayers to heaven when I needed wisdom or discernment in a conversation and even suggested He might find me a parking place when I was running late. Was this communication with God really prayer? I decided to search the Scriptures for some insights.

After even a cursory reading of Acts, it is clear the early Christians were not sedentary folks. They were busy making tents, teaching, fishing, caring for their families, ministering to the faithful, tending their crops, and running their businesses. They had little free time. Yet the Scriptures are filled with accounts of them praying continually, night and day.

In the Old Testament are numerous accounts of God's faithful servants communicating with Him from cities and mountaintops, from the bottom of muddy pits and the murky darkness of caves, from the royal courts of Egypt and Israel. And from the pen of

Hear, O Lord, and answer me, for I am poor and needy. Guard my life, for I am devoted to You. You are my God; save Your servant who trusts in You. Have mercy on me, O Lord, for I call to You all day long. Bring joy to Your servant, for to You, O Lord, I lift up my soul. You are forgiving and good, O Lord, abounding in love to all who call to You. Psalm 86:1–5

Because Your love is better than life, my lips will glorify You. I will praise You as long as I live, and in Your name I will lift up my hands. My soul will be satisfied as with the richest of foods; with singing lips my mouth will praise You. On my bed I remember You; I think of You through the watches of the night. Because You are my help, I sing in the shadow of Your wings. My soul clings to You; Your right hand upholds me. Psalm 63:3–8

David, we are encouraged to come to God for whatever we need, from wherever we are:

God is constant and ever watchful of us, His children. And as His children, we may come to Him at any time for any reason. When we are not able to kneel in our private place of prayer, we may still freely run to Him, bringing our joys and pain, our cares and hopes with confidence. He is a Father who is always accessible and never too busy to listen.

Scripture for Further Meditation

The Lord is near to all who call on Him, to all who call on Him in truth. Psalm 145:18

Practical Application

Talk to God throughout your day. In the morning, submit your plans for the day to His direction. As you go about your work, seek His guidance before making a decision or suggestion. When you experience a joy or victory, thank and praise Him for His goodness and grace. In your relationships, seek His insights into people and their behavior. As you prepare to fall asleep, review your day with Him and seek His forgiveness where it is needed. Constant conversation with the Lord keeps us in tune with His will and heightens our sensitivity to His leading in our lives.

Prayer

Dear Father, keep me ever mindful of Your presence with me each moment of the day. When I speak or act, let me first consider what You would have me say or do. As I touch the lives of others, may I do it with the leading of Your Holy Spirit. Thank You for Your constant presence in my life. Amen.

Broken Promises!

MY FOURTH-GRADE DAUGHTER burst through the front door, dropped her backpack on the slate floor, and stomped up the stairs. I heard the door to her bedroom slam and I sighed. It seemed every day held some new frustration for her. Friendships among the girls in her class were in a constant state of flux and someone was usually left with ruffled feathers or hurt feelings. Nine- and 10-year-olds live in a sweet-and-sour world—sweet one moment and sour the next.

I grabbed a couple of oatmeal cookies and headed up the stairs. After knocking on her door, I pushed it open a few inches.

"Would a cookie make things better?" I inquired.

"I don't know," came the sullen reply.

I took that as an affirmative and walked into her room, placed the cookie on her pillow next to her nose, and sat in the rocker munching my own cookie.

"So, not a great day, huh?"

She groaned and sat up, cross-legged on her bed, picked up the cookie, and took a bite. "You wouldn't believe what happened today. Maryanne, who was supposed to be my best friend, is planning a sleep-over and she didn't invite me. AND," she continued when I opened my mouth to make a comment, "she made a point of inviting Kate, who I happen to know she doesn't even like. AND," she added, holding up her hand to fend off any remarks I was about to offer, "she absolutely promised me I was going to be invit-ed to her next sleepover." I waited for a minute to make certain she was finished. She wasn't.

"Last month she promised me we would go to the bowling alley together and she kept putting it off and making excuses and we never did go. Then just last week she promised me I could borrow her Winnie the Pooh sweatshirt, but then she said she couldn't find it. But I know that wasn't true because she wore it on Friday! Why does she keep making promises if she isn't going to keep them?" She stuffed the rest of the cookie in her mouth. Since her mouth was full, I thought it safe to venture a remark.

"Well, why do you keep believing her if she keeps breaking her promises?"

She shook her head and swallowed the cookie. "You don't get it, Mom. She's supposed to be my best friend. Best friends trust each other."

I smiled at her earnest expression. "Anne, best friends keep their promises."

"Not always," she countered.

"What do you mean?"

"Well, you said we were all going to the zoo last weekend, but we didn't. And Dad promised to bring home that special paper for my science project and he didn't." She crossed her arms and looked at me. "And your parents are supposed to be your very best friends."

"Honey, it rained all weekend and Daddy was just busy and forgot the paper." Couldn't she see the difference between these situations and that with her friend?

"Well, still," she wavered a bit, then raised her chin, "a promise is supposed to be kept."

I looked at her sitting stubbornly on the bed and realized she had a point. Promises *are* supposed to be kept. But who can ever keep all of them? They are easy to make and often, due to circumstances or our own failings, very easy to break as well. Parents and children, husbands and wives, governments and citizens—all of us make and break promises to each other. How could I help her understand the value of promise keeping when all the examples I had to offer were flawed? All the examples but one.

"Come on downstairs," I suggested. "I want to show you something."

Curious, she followed me down the stairs and into the family room. There I took up my Bible and invited her to sit beside me on the couch. We read passages from Genesis, outlining God's wonderful promises to Abraham and Sarah. We talked for awhile about God's promises and how He always kept them, no matter what.

"I guess you're right, Anne. Sometimes the people

we love don't keep their promises, but we can always trust that God will." She snuggled close and gave me a hug and I kissed the top of her head. And I recalled a promise God had made to me long ago when I had prayed for a daughter.

Reflections

If we are honorable, we intend to keep our promises, to tell the truth, and to be trustworthy. We also hope others will do the same. Our good intentions, however, are often not sufficient. Sometimes we have a change of heart about a promise we've made and decide we no longer wish to keep it. Sometimes poor health or other circumstances interfere with keeping promises. Sometimes we make promises assuming we have the power to keep them when we do not. As human beings we learn to accept the inevitability of broken promises from one another. As children of God however, we have the assurance that our heavenly Father will never break a promise.

Throughout the Scriptures God reveals Himself as utterly trustworthy. He is the Keeper of Promises. And nowhere is this characteristic more evident than in the ancient story of Abraham, the father of the Jewish nation.

At age 75, Abram had a comfortable life with his wife and their extended family in the plains of Haran.

> *"Leave your country, your people and your father's household and go to the land I will show you.*
>
> *"I will make you into a great nation and I will bless you; I will make your name great, and you will be a blessing. I will bless those who bless you, and whoever curses you I will curse; and all peoples on earth will be blessed through you."*
> Genesis 12:1–3

Then one day the Lord spoke to Abram in an avalanche of promises:

Abram believed God's promises and throughout his life saw them fulfilled. God blessed him with land, children, wealth, a new name, and a heritage through which we still experience blessing several millennia after Abraham's death. The wonder of it is not that God made such wonderful promises, but that He perfectly keeps them.

When I consider the fallibility of the world in which I live and the people I know—including myself—it is easy for me to become cynical. It may cause me to question if anyone keeps promises anymore and if it is even possible to know the truth for sure. It is the same attitude expressed by my 9-year-old daughter. And just as I pointed her back to the Word of God, I must continually go there myself. In those sacred pages I find the answers to my doubts not in a creed, but in a Person. John describes Him this way: "The Word became flesh and made His dwelling among us. We have seen His glory, the glory of the One and Only, who came from the Father, full of grace and truth" (John 1:14). And Jesus describes Himself: "I am the way and the truth and the life" (John 14:6).

While it is discouraging when others fail to keep their promises, both my daughter and I found encouragement as we read and realized again the promise-keeping nature of God. As we trust in Him, we are assured that, fixed upon the Lord, our hopes will never be disappointed.

Scripture for Further Meditation

Let us hold unswervingly to the hope we profess, for He who promised is faithful. Hebrews 10:23

Practical Application

As you read through the Scriptures, keep a notebook of verses containing the promises of God. When you feel discouraged or disappointed by people or circumstances, read your list of promises, thanking God for His faithfulness. Make an effort to be careful about the promises you make and seek God's help in keeping your commitments to others.

Prayer

Father, I confess I have not always been faithful in keeping my promises to others. Forgive me for those times I have broken my word. Thank You for Your perfect promise expressed through my Savior, Jesus Christ. Give me the faith and strength to follow His example in all I do and say. Amen.

Don't Worry, Mom

"MOM, DO YOU THINK I SHOULD TAKE MY SWIM SUIT?"
My older son stood in the doorway, waving a pair of
trunks above his head.

"Shhh," I whispered. "Just a minute and I'll be
with you."

I put the baby down, turned out the lights in her
room, and quietly closed the door. She whimpered a
few times, then quieted herself. I knew she'd be
asleep in a minute or two, safely snuggled in her
crib.

My son dangled his swimsuit a few inches from
my face. "What do you think?"

"I think you should be a little bit more patient," I
said, trying not to sound cross as we entered his bedroom.

"Oh, Mom, this is going to be so cool. I can't
believe I get to be on a Navy ship for a whole week
and hang out with all the guys and eat donuts and
pizza whenever I want and play video games all the
time and go to bed whenever I want and, best of all,
miss school!" He finished his liturgy with a victory
yell as he leapt on his bed.

"Well, you still have to do your homework and I'm sure Dad will have something to say about all the rest of those things." I looked at him and smiled at his unbridled joy.

"Yeah, but Dad and I understand each other, Mom. We're both guys."

That, I thought, was what worried me the most. Forget the routines, nutritious food, and schedules. Sending my 8-year-old off to spend a week on the high seas gave me more than a little trepidation. But my husband and I had discussed this adventure at length, and Josh had been anticipating it for months. In a few days I would drive him to Los Angeles where he would board a plane for Honolulu. There, his dad, the Executive Officer on a warship, would pick him up for a week-long "Tiger Cruise" back to the West Coast, culminating a seven-month deployment in the Far East. It was the adventure of a lifetime and I understood his excitement. But I kept thinking about how young he was and how easy it would be for him to fall overboard. Then there were all those young sailors on the ship and who knows what kind of interesting information they might impart. I trusted my husband to watch out for Josh, but I knew he had a job to do. How could he keep an eye on our son all the time? At night my dreams were filled with storms at sea and deafening engine rooms, belching super-heated steam.

"Did I tell you Dad said in his last letter I might get to shoot the antiaircraft guns?" Standing on his bed, Josh aimed at the window and loudly "shot down" a fleet of enemy planes. I groaned and stuck a few extra pair of clean socks and underwear in the suitcase.

The morning of his departure, Josh was up at dawn, dressed and eating a bowl of cereal before I had fixed coffee. His suitcase stood by the door with his plane ticket tucked securely under the handle. As I ate and dressed, then dropped the other two children off with a neighbor, Josh could hardly remain still. This would be a time of firsts for him—and for me as well. All he saw was the adventure, the excitement and in his eyes the world was a place full of wonderful possibilities. In addition to these things, I saw the dangers and uncertainties and I knew the world was also a frightening place. I saw how small he was, how trusting and naive.

The airline agent checked the tickets and invited Josh to board early. Without a glance at me he grabbed his backpack and headed eagerly for the plane.

My eyes filled with tears and I called, "Have a great trip, Honey!"

He spun around and dashed back, tackling me with a big hug. "Oh, man, I was so excited I almost forgot to say good-bye! Don't worry about me, Mom. Dad will be there. See you later!" He gave me an awkward kiss on the cheek and dashed off down the jet-way, eager to begin his adventure.

I waited and watched the plane take off, thinking about the unknowns still ahead of him. And then I recalled his farewell and realized my young son had unknowingly taught me an important lesson that day. He stated the reason for his confidence in four simple words: "Dad will be there." In all my worry and apprehension, I had overlooked the one truth that would have calmed my fears: My Father will be there.

Reflections

As a mother it is easy to become anxious about all the challenges facing my children. When they are babies, they are so totally dependent upon my loving protection. Their world is circumscribed by the boundaries of our home. There I feel I can protect and insulate them from the dangers outside our door. But the time soon comes when they must venture beyond my boundaries into the world. And the world is not a very friendly place for children. As a loving mother, what can I do? How can I let them go?

One of my favorite Bible characters faced just such a dilemma and in her words I find the answers to my questions. She was a woman who, like me, had longed for a child for years. After a time of fervent prayer, God answered Hannah's request:

So in the course of time Hannah conceived and gave birth to a son. She named him Samuel, saying, "Because I asked the LORD for him."
1 Samuel 1:20

Hannah made a vow to the Lord before the child was even conceived, promising to give her son back to the Lord. How difficult it must have been once she held that tiny boy in her arms to consider giving him up. Remembering the emptiness of her arms before Samuel's birth, I cannot imagine her feelings as she anticipated his absence. Who would have blamed her for breaking her vow? But Hannah was a woman of great faith and resolve.

After he was weaned, she took the boy with her, young as he was, along with a three-year-old bull, an ephah of flour and a skin of wine, and brought him to the house of the LORD at Shiloh. When they had slaughtered the bull, they brought the boy to Eli, and she said to him, "As surely as you live, my lord, I am the woman who stood here beside you praying to the LORD. I prayed for this child, and the LORD has granted me what I asked of Him. So now I give Him to the LORD. For his whole life he will be given over to the LORD." And he worshiped the LORD there. 1 Samuel 1:24–28

It might sound at first like this was a safe place for a little one to be and Hannah could rest easy knowing Samuel was in the care of those in the Lord's service. If you read on however, it becomes evident the situation at Samuel's new home was less than perfect. Eli, the head priest at the temple in

Shiloh, was not particularly nurturing. Listen to what the Scriptures say about his two sons: "Eli's sons were wicked men; they had no regard for the LORD" (1 Samuel 2:12).

Every time I read Hannah's story I try to imagine her feelings. Her precious little boy was to live in a cavernous religious temple surrounded by evil men. How could she leave him there at the age of 3 or 4, knowing this? I believe Hannah gives us the answer in the first verses of her beautiful prayer:

> *My heart rejoices in the LORD; in the LORD my horn is lifted high.*
> *My mouth boasts over my enemies, for I delight in Your deliverance.*
> *There is no one holy like the LORD; there is no one besides You; there is no Rock like our God.*
> *1 Samuel 2:1–2*

Hannah knew that wherever her Samuel went, God was there. She didn't trust in circumstances or other people or even her love as a mother. God had given her this child and she had given him back to God. And God was totally trustworthy.

Every time I send one of my children off to a new situation—kindergarten, summer camp, a trip across the country, college—I think of Hannah's prayer. Although I cannot know or protect them from the dangers they may encounter, I still have confidence they are in God's care. As my 8-year-old son helped me realize, their Father will be there.

Scripture for Further Meditation

For I am convinced that neither death nor life, neither angels nor demons, neither the present nor the future, nor any powers, neither height nor depth, nor anything else in all creation, will be able to separate us from the love of God that is in Christ Jesus our Lord. Romans 8:35

Practical Application

Pray for and with your children or grandchildren as they face challenges at school and in their communities. Encourage them to trust in God's guidance and protection by sharing experiences you have had when God guided and protected you. Help them memorize Scriptures that speak of God's loving care. Write notes reminding them of your confidence that God loves them and is with them. Build a heritage of confidence in the Lord's unfailing presence.

Prayer

Dear Jesus, when I am fearful for my children and tempted to worry about them, please remind me that You love and care for them even more than I do. Help me entrust them to Your keeping, knowing that Your love will never fail. You, O Lord, are the Rock on which I stand. Amen.

The Uniform

DURING HIS SOPHOMORE YEAR IN HIGH SCHOOL,
Doug decided he wanted to try out for the football
team. We lived in Hawaii at the time and practices
started in the summer. The team worked out from
8:00 in the morning until 11:00, then came back to
the field for two more hours of practice late in the
afternoon. Most days the temperature was in the 80s
and the humidity was high. The coach had the boys
running laps, lifting weights, and doing exercises
until some of them dropped in exhaustion. A few of
them quit but our son kept going.

"Coach says being on a team is more than just
showing up," Doug explained one day when discussing the rigorous workouts. "You have to have
heart. You have to want to be part of the team more
than anything else. Nobody gets to wear the uniform
unless they're willing to sacrifice for it. Coach says
we have to decide to be winners before we ever play
our first game. Winning is an attitude, Mom, not just
a score."

I agreed that Coach certainly was inspirational.
"When will you find out who is on the team?" I

inquired.

"Not until just before school starts. Coach wants to keep us hungry."

"I see," I remarked as he poured himself a third bowl of cereal for an afternoon snack. "He seems to be doing a great job."

We continued to be inspired by Coach's words of wisdom until the week of team selection arrived. Day after day boys were cut from the team until, on the last day, the team roster was posted by the locker room door. When our son burst into the house after practice that final day, I knew he had made the team.

"This is just so cool," he kept repeating. "We had a team meeting after practice and Coach filled us in on what we need to know. We have to keep our grades up because if your GPA drops, you could be kicked off the team. And he said when we wear the uniform we have to remember we represent the whole team and our school. Everyone will know we're Radford Rams. We get to wear our team shirts to school on game days."

I smiled as he passed along more nuggets from Coach. His eyes shone with excitement and pride. The weeks of practice in the hot sun had left him tanned and muscular. He held himself with a new confidence, won by the trials of training and the knowledge he had worked hard to earn something of value. Right now, he knew it and we knew it. When he put on the uniform, everyone else would know it.

The Saturday before school started, Doug picked up the coveted football uniform. He lugged it home in a big athletic bag and laid the pieces on his bed one by one. When I walked by his room, I spotted him sitting on the bed wearing his black and red jersey while polishing his helmet with car wax. The golden ram horns curling along the sides of the helmet gleamed.

I poked my head in the door. "Is that so the opposing players will just slide away from you as you smack them with your head?" I asked.

He looked up and grinned. "Yeah, right, Mom. Coach says we should look as good as we want to play. Look sharp; be sharp."

I glanced at the piles of clothes, books, and sports equipment littering Doug's floor and suggested Coach might want to come on over for a look around. My son just shook his head and continued buffing his helmet.

That fall the football uniform had a prominent place in our son's wardrobe. On game days he wore his jersey to school and between games he took care to remove any scuff marks from the helmet. When the team ran out onto the field, they exemplified what their coach called "Rampride."

Being identified with the team by a uniform meant more to Doug than just having a special shirt to wear. It was a visual aid conveying all the values and hard work of the team, a testimony to the choices they had made individually and together and a sign of their willingness to follow the leadership of their coach.

One day as I tossed his football jersey in the dryer, I wondered what would happen if there were a special uniform for Christians. If we were awarded that uniform according to our dedication and devotion to the team, and the diligence with which we follow our Coach, how many of us would qualify to wear it?

Reflections

Being identified with a cause has become very popular in our culture. T-shirts emblazoned with logos or slogans adorn the faithful followers of everything from sports teams to political parties. Buttons and ribbons symbolizing the wearers' sympathies are found everywhere from school campuses to glitzy awards shows in Hollywood and New York. And bumper stickers have become an art form declaring views both secular and sacred.

Unfortunately these kinds of declarations aren't always as sincere as one might hope. I recall an incident where a car ahead of me had a "Honk if You Love Jesus" sticker on the bumper and the driver made an obscene gesture out the window at a passing motorist who gave him a friendly toot! Perhaps this type of mixed message comes from the sender's reluctance to really consider the consequence of the choice he or she makes. Just as my son had to consider the cost and choose to accept the requirements of the team before he was allowed to wear the coveted football uniform, I too must decide what it means to carry the name of Christian.

In the Old Testament, we read about Joshua preparing to die. He had faithfully followed the directives of both Moses and God, and the tribes of Israel were dwelling in peace and prosperity. He gathered representatives from the 12 tribes of Israel at Shechem and delivered his last address as their leader. He reminded them of God's goodness over the preceding decades as their families escaped from the slavery of Egypt, wandered in the lonely desert, and experienced victory in the Promised Land. He concluded his stirring sermon with a challenge:

"Now fear the LORD and serve Him with all faithfulness. Throw away the gods your forefathers worshiped beyond the River and in Egypt, and serve the LORD. But if serving the LORD seems undesirable to you, then choose for yourselves this day whom you will serve, whether the gods your forefathers served beyond the River, or the gods of the Amorites, in whose land you are living. But as for me and my household, we will serve the LORD."
Joshua 24:14–15

Joshua knew making a choice for one way of life necessitated going against other ways of life. If the Israelites wanted to serve God, they needed to get rid of the things that impeded them, commit themselves to faithful worship, and strengthen their resolve to follow the Lord at all costs. Joshua knew the importance of wholehearted dedication and he declared his intention quite clearly. He didn't care what anyone else thought. He had worked hard, had experienced the discipline of his training, and proudly wore the uniform of God's servant.

Is this how I approach my faith? Many times I find it easier to travel the road of faith incognito, identifying myself as a Christian only when I'm sure it will be convenient or inoffensive to others. It is easy to declare my devotion to Christ at church or in a Bible study, but not so comfortable at work or in my neighborhood. And what if the people I'm with are openly hostile to my faith? Isn't it just less trouble to keep quiet? Although I often cover my intentions with high-sounding motives, the truth is I sometimes choose to leave my "religious uniform" at home on game days and sit on the sidelines, uninvolved and safe.

Scripture for Further Meditation

Finally, be strong in the Lord and in His mighty power. Put on the full armor of God so that you can take your stand against the devil's schemes. Ephesians 6:10–11

Practical Application

Read Ephesians 6:12–18. After each item in the "Believer's Uniform" listed below, write how that part might help you live out your choice to be on God's team:

Belt of truth:

Breastplate of righteousness:

Shoes of the Gospel of peace:

Shield of faith:

Helmet of salvation:

Sword of the Spirit:

Prayer

Dear Father, forgive me for my willingness to be identified with You only when it's convenient and costs me nothing. Help me choose each day to put on the uniform of faith and stand with other believers as we work together for the victory of righteousness over evil. Thank You for Your constant guidance and encouragement given through the Spirit and the Word. Amen.

The Vacation

WHEN MY HUSBAND DECIDED TO RETIRE after 28 years in the military, we knew we'd be experiencing some dramatic changes in our lives. He accepted a position with a private company and we'd be moving to a different home—this time permanently. Our lives would no longer be circumscribed by the regulations and rhythms of military protocol. Our children were at transition points in their lives too. Our oldest, Josh, was preparing to begin a career in computer science. Doug was eager to start his first year of college. And our daughter, Anne, anticipated the beginning of high school.

"What we need to do is take one last family trip together," I mused one evening. "Only this time it should be a real vacation." In all our years of travel, the family had taken many trips together but they were always incorporated with a move. They were rarely relaxing.

"Why don't we see if the kids want to drive from Seattle to California? We can let them choose the things they want to see along the way," my husband offered. I knew he was probably motivated by a desire to road test his newly acquired van as much as his longing for family togetherness, but why quibble about technicalities?

The kids were enthusiastic about our proposal, even the oldest who usually opted for his own space and solitude when given a choice. I knew it would probably be the last time we would all spend two weeks together in close proximity and looked forward to our adventure with great anticipation.

After months of planning, we piled into the van one brilliant August morning and headed south. Our only rule for the trip was no whining. Each of us had input on the itinerary and no one was to rain on anyone else's parade. It didn't take long to settle into a routine. I often read the paper aloud in the morning as we drove along the freeway. The kids listened to their CDs to pass the time and we stopped to observe some interesting land feature or spectacular vista as we drove through mountains and forests. There was lots of good-natured teasing and joking as we recalled past experiences as a family. The children had great fun comparing notes on family life at different stages and ages and we chuckled as the boys shared strategies for their sister to employ when she faced dealing with us in her high school years.

The days were long and golden, filled with stops at the ocean, theme parks, a zoo, and some of the places we had lived years earlier. Our daughter saw the hospital where she was born and her first home. Doug found the corner where he had crashed his bike into a cactus when he was learning to ride, and Josh revisited the hamburger joint where he and his dad spent special times together when he was in second grade.

One evening my husband and I watched the three of them cavorting together in the hotel pool. "Did you ever think they'd have so much fun together?" I asked remembering how they teased and bickered with one another when they were younger.

"Each one is an individual," he remarked thoughtfully. "But now, instead of emphasizing their differences, they appreciate them and enjoy what they have in common."

I looked at the children again. Josh, our scientist, saw life in absolutes and tended to be a pessimist. Doug, the philosopher, found the various nuances of people and places a fascinating puzzle and delighted in finding humor in just about everything. Anne, the romantic, could lose herself in music or literature and yearned for a life filled with fairy-tale drama. I marveled how the same genetic material and environment produced such variety. And yet it was that variety that produced the rich texture of our family.

I reached over and took my husband's hand as I realized his observation held the key to not only family harmony but the integrity of any group of people. As we mature, we learn to appreciate our differences rather than be divided by them. And in doing so we see each other as assets instead of liabilities.

Reflections

In any family, church, or community, it is easy to focus on differences and be irritated by them. In a family, where we live together in close proximity, these irritations can escalate into battles. But as I learned on our vacation, as we grow, so should our willingness to overlook or even delight in our diversity. When this happens, the strengths in one complement the weaknesses in another and the whole family is blessed.

In choosing His disciples, Jesus affirmed this principle. He certainly chose a diverse group of men whose differences could have led to outright warfare without His loving direction and tender care.

One of those days Jesus went out to a mountainside to pray, and spent the night praying to God. When morning came, He called His disciples to Him and chose twelve of them whom He also designated apostles: Simon (whom He named Peter), his brother Andrew, James, John, Philip, Bartholomew, Matthew, Thomas, James son of Alphaeus, Simon who was called the Zealot, Judas son of James, and Judas Iscariot, who became a traitor. Luke 6:12–16

What a diverse group!

There were two sets of brothers and several men who had never met, fishermen and scholars, religious zealots and secular businessmen, a political rightwinger, and a tax collector with ties to Rome; doubters and true believers, patient men as well as the impetuous, faithful friends, and even a traitorous thief. Knowing all this, Jesus prayerfully chose these 12 to be in His inner circle during His earthly ministry. Perhaps He knew their differences would force them to look to God for unity and purpose. I suspect He saw the strengths and weaknesses of each as representative of mankind and drew them together because He knew they could, with His leadership and inspiration, reach all humanity.

Placing us in close proximity to those different from ourselves seems to be part of God's plan. Jesus demonstrated that not only in His choice of disciples, but in His dealings with all people. He honored the prostitute in the home of a Pharisee. He welcomed the leper in the midst of those who considered him unclean. He held little children while important dignitaries clamored for His attention. And finally, the King of Heaven allowed Himself to be crucified between two convicted criminals. Christ never called us to be the same; He prayed for us to be one.

It is easy and perhaps very natural to want to be with those who are most like us. People who think like I do rarely challenge my views. They appreciate the same things I do and echo my own predispositions and prejudices. I feel comfortable when I'm with them. But there's a danger in staying in the company of clones. It tends to make me self-righteous and judgmental and it eliminates the necessity for me to mature.

If Christ in His infinite wisdom consecrated diversity, shouldn't we work to at least appreciate our differences? Looking at my children, I see how their uniqueness helped me grow as a person. In dealing with one's strong will, I had to learn to be firm yet fair. With another's sensitivity I needed to master the art of guiding the will without bruising the spirit. Challenged often by their questions and novel ideas, I am continually forced to evaluate my views. I am drawn to the Word for wisdom and to the Spirit for guidance. In the process I pray that I am becoming the woman God intended me to be.

Scripture for Further Meditation

"My prayer is not for them alone.
I pray also for those who will believe in Me
through their message, that all of them may be one,
Father, just as You are in Me and I am in You. May
they also be in us so that the world may believe that
You have sent Me." John 17:20–21

Practical Application

Write down each of your children's names on a piece of paper. Under each name, write the character traits and talents that make him or her unique. In your prayer time, give thanks each day for one of these qualities. Instead of being critical or nagging the child to be more like you, ask God for ideas about how to express appreciation for the diversity that child brings to your family. You may also wish to do this exercise with other family members and acquaintances, lessening the expression of critical feelings and strengthening the bonds of unity.

Prayer

Dear Jesus, I know You relished the diversity in the world You created. I confess I often am critical of those who differ from me. Help me see others with Your eyes and appreciate them for the unique gifts they offer. Thank You for accepting and loving me. Give me the grace to accept and love others in Your name. Amen.